HOW TO EARN A COLLEGE DEGREE:

WHEN YOU THINK YOU ARE   Too Old

                           Too Busy

                           Too Broke

                           Too Scared

An Educational Planning Guide for Adult Learners

Third Edition

Published by
Educational Advisory Services, Inc.
www.E-A-S.com

EDUCATIONAL
ADVISORY
SERVICES

Author
E. Faith Ivery, Ed.D.

2003

Library of Congress Catalog Card Number 00-00000
ISBN 0-9636496-1-2
ISSN 0000-0000

Published by:

EDUCATIONAL ADVISORY SERVICES, INC.®
10505 North 69th Street, Suite #1300
Scottsdale, AZ 85253
(480) 922-8986
www.E-A-S.com

Printed in the United States of America
PrintFast, Inc. Scottsdale, Arizona
(480) 948-4734

DISCLAIMER: The purpose of this activity book is to provide information
in regard to the subject matter covered. The author, and Educational Advisory Services, Inc.
shall have neither liability nor responsibility to any person or entity with respect to any loss or
damage caused or alleged to be caused directly or indirectly by the information contained in this book.

TABLE OF CONTENTS

INTRODUCTION

Think about going to college and you probably picture a place--a college campus in whose buildings you will attend all your classes until you accumulate enough knowledge and credits to earn your degree. This image of higher education has been with us for a long time - ivy walls, fraternities, football, lecture halls. It thrived in early movies starring Ronald Reagan as "Joe College" and June Allyson as "the Co-ed." If you remember this, then you <u>are</u> an adult learner!

This image of College is traditional, innocent, romantic, and wrong. Technology, a changing economy, and rapid social change are bringing adults back to colleges to complete their degrees, seek an education that never before was possible, or retrain for a new career. Almost half of all national college enrollments are classified as adult students! This equates to about 8.7 million adult learners – and by the year 2012 about 9.7 million adults over the age of 22 will be going "back to school" for a college degree*. Lifelong learning is not a trend, but a necessity.

Not surprisingly, colleges have had to change to keep in step with the times. You may now attend college classes in an office building or a hotel. Classes are offered on weekends, in the evenings, or in compact units of 5-week sessions. You may earn credit by taking tests, enrolling in courses offered through correspondence, television or your computer, and by documenting life experience.

If you are an adult contemplating returning to college, or if you are taking courses, this book is for you. This guidebook will help you make personal choices about your life's direction and educational planning. Adult learners often require alternative ways to learn and earn college degrees. Options for college-bound adult learners will be examined for ways to create a personalized educational plan that meets your learning style, lifestyle, and budget.

Each chapter will focus on a specific aspect of successful educational planning. Your participation in the activities provided in each chapter will increase your self-awareness and lead to a final plan of action. This book will help your planning for Undergraduate or Graduate degrees.

"College Education: It's Not Just For Kids Anymore"

*The U.S. Department of Education, National Center for Education Statistics (NCES); May 2002

CHAPTER ONE — LEARNING ABOUT YOU

Assessing Your Educational Goals

"Which way do I go?"

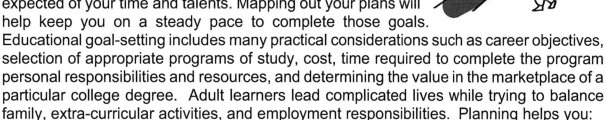

The first step in returning to higher education involves setting goals to help assure success. Assessing your educational goals and options gives you a clearer picture of what will be expected of your time and talents. Mapping out your plans will help keep you on a steady pace to complete those goals. Educational goal-setting includes many practical considerations such as career objectives, selection of appropriate programs of study, cost, time required to complete the program personal responsibilities and resources, and determining the value in the marketplace of a particular college degree. Adult learners lead complicated lives while trying to balance family, extra-curricular activities, and employment responsibilities. Planning helps you:

>**REVIEW where you are now**
>**DECIDE where you want to go**
>**DISCOVER how furthering your education will help you WIN!**

Approach your continuing education as a consumer. The degree is the "product", and the colleges/universities are the "providers". You certainly wouldn't buy the first car you saw in the showroom without making sure the vehicle had the features you were looking for and a price within your budget. Selecting a college/university is no different. Shop wisely and carefully to find the school and program that best meet your needs.

Determining your career goals is the essential first step to planning your continued education. If you have completed a career assessment, your educational goals probably are much clearer to you. This guidebook focuses on educational planning, which will help ensure that the particular program of study you choose will be relevant and useful to your career goals. There are many books, tapes, and videos that can help you make decisions about the direction of your career and answer the ultimate question - What do I want to be when I grow up?

We strongly recommend contacting professional career counselors who can administer various assessment instruments (not tests!) to determine your interests, values, and skills. Professionals will work with you to bring out your feelings and use practical information to narrow your fields of interest. If you are able to pinpoint your career goals, it will be easier to identify educational goals that provide the knowledge and credentials you need to succeed. You can contact your local community college for inexpensive career assessment and counseling, or select a professional career counselor in private practice from the telephone book. Many companies also have career counselors and career centers for their employees.

A college degree by itself does not guarantee you a better job or higher earnings. It is only part of the package you bring to an employer. However, a degree is becoming necessary for promotion, job retention, and increased marketability in these changing economic times. In addition, college study offers personal and social rewards by increasing self-esteem and developing analytical and communication skills.

Employers are impressed with degrees in a specific area of study (Accounting, Engineering, Education, others), but are also interested in employees with well-developed *liberal arts skills.* Studies have shown that employees with liberal arts skills tend to rise further in an organization than those with narrower education and training. The following chart identifies liberal arts skills and shows how they transfer to the workplace. Think about the job you now hold or the job you wish to have in the future. Where do you use or could you use these skills? Look at the chart on the following pages and use this information to complete this exercise.

 EXERCISE: Liberal Arts & Skills

Complete the following grid using either your current position or the position you hope to attain in the future.

First, identify 3 specific tasks you perform (or think you would perform in a future job) using these skills. Then, select which skills or competencies you have gained from a specific task from the chart on page 7.

An example follows. Then, complete your own chart. You can continue on a separate sheet of paper to extend this exercise and define more skills gained from specific tasks.

Current or future position	Skill/Competency	Specific Task
Fund-raiser	Written communication	Prepare mo. donor report

1.

2.

3.

LIBERAL ARTS SKILLS

Skills and competencies	Abilities	Transferability to Marketplace	Course work which stimulates development
Written Communication/ Verbal Communication	Organize thoughts Conduct research Articulate ideas Defend a position	Report writing Memo/letter Meeting Presentation	Communications Composition Literature Speech
Argumentation	Think critically Discern impact of ideas Formulate problems clearly Disclose hidden assumptions and values	Readily respond to issues Think on your feet Present and evaluate information one-on-one or in a team	Composition Economics History Philosophy Political Science Speech
Analytical	Problem solve Think logically Understand and use statistics	Analyze trends Present/Evaluate results Imagine possibilities	Linguistics Literature Philosophy Mathematics Sciences
Foreign Language	Appreciate cultural diversity Better understand English language Communicate with other cultures	Interaction with diverse client cultures Knowledge of client/colleague cultures	French German Arabic Japanese Russian...
Understanding of individual and cultural differences	Relate to others Set aside bias Flexibility Adaptability	Supervision Collegial relations Public/Client Relations	Anthropology Psychology Sociology
Historical Perspective	Understand and predict historical trends and relationships Appreciate cultural diversity Understand social issues and movements	Supervision Dealing with colleagues Affirmative action Employee benefits	Economics History Literature Political Science
Aesthetic Appreciation	Understanding that art reflects historical and social movements Understanding that art reflects sensitivities/issues of other people/cultures	Professional/Social interactions Understanding of your client or the consumer market	Applied Art/Music Art/Music History General Humanities Literature
Fundamental Scientific Concepts	Problem solve Think logically Understand and use statistics	Quantify, evaluate and synthesize information Propose solutions	Anthropology Mathematics Sciences

Chart created by K. Crapo and K. Wittkopp while employed by the University of Michigan-Dearborn.

You may have a very specific goal in mind. For example, you may want to earn a bachelor's degree in Management so that you will be eligible for a promotion at your place of employment. This type of "fine-tuning" will increase your effectiveness in educational planning. Complete the following exercises even if your educational objectives are clear to you.

 EXERCISES: Fine Tune Your Dreams .....

I. What do you want to be doing five years from now?

A.   My personal/family goals are:

B.   My professional goals are as follows:
I hope to have a position as:

The job duties/responsibilities I will be performing are (Describe the job tasks you hope to be performing):

I plan to live (Describe the geographic location where you wish to live. Be as specific as possible. Will this require a move?):

I plan to work in (Do you plan to work for a large or small company? For yourself? In an office? In your home?):

C.   My financial goals are (Salary, savings, investments, material goods):

II. What are your reasons for wanting a college degree? Enrichment? Self-esteem? Job promotion? Fun? List as many reasons as you can.

A.

B.

C.

D.

E.

3. What can a degree do for me? (Check those responses with which you agree)

A. _____ A degree is required for advancement in my organization.
B. _____ I don't need a degree for my job; I just want one for me.
C. _____ A degree will give me new knowledge and skills.
D. _____ A degree can make me eligible for increased salary.
E. _____ I need a degree to attain my career goals.
F. _____ A degree will make me more marketable if I lose my job.
G. _____ A degree can broaden my views of the world.
H. _____ I will serve as a positive role model for my children.
I. _____ A degree can help me prepare for job changes.
J. _____ A degree will help me feel less inferior or disadvantaged.

Assessing Your Learning Style

Another important part of planning your education includes defining how YOU learn best. Throughout grade school, high school and college Americans are tested for aptitude, IQ, abilities, and admissions. Has anyone ever asked, "How do you learn best?" Usually, the answer is "NO".

Exploring how you learn best will help you select appropriate majors, courses, and programs that match to your career goals. Many times learners feel they have failed if they receive a "C" or below, or had to drop a course, or change a program of study. You must realize that most learners cannot excel in every subject or field. Pick those areas of study that fit your learning abilities— at least at the start of your program. Keep in mind that as an adult you have already learned to somewhat adapt your learning style to accommodate the environment in which you find yourself. This flexibility is one of the advantages adult learners bring to the classroom.

Perhaps in the past you did poorly in a course. Have you ever stopped to consider the reasons why? If it is not for obvious reasons, such as cutting class or not studying, what could have caused the problem? You may have been in the wrong course or the instructor's teaching method may have been at odds with your learning style. Have you ever been in a seminar, training class or college course that others thought was excellent and you thought was boring or confusing? This is because there are many teaching methods and learning styles.

Dr. David Kolb, at Case Western Reserve University in Cleveland, Ohio, observed that after his class some students would rush up to him and tell him that the lecture had been interesting, well-organized, well-presented, and informative. Other students seemed to have the opposite reaction. All of the students had attended the same class on the same day at the same time and listened to the same material. This led Dr. Kolb to study individual learning styles. He developed an inventory (not a test!) to assess an individual's preferred learning style--that is, how a person deals with ideas, situations, and new information. We strongly recommend finding a school in your area that offers the Learning Style Inventory by Dr. Kolb or contact the Hay Group, Inc. – they distribute the LSI (**www.haygroup.com**). You can take the assessment online, which includes a self-scoring booklet of information you can print.

Here is a brief outline of Dr. Kolb's model for learning to give you an understanding for the type of learner you are:

First, learning is a process. Our style changes throughout life and <u>no single way of learning is better than another</u>. The ideal is to be a flexible and adaptable learner to meet the demands of a learning situation. However, everyone has learning strengths, weaknesses, and preferences.

In this model there are four different types of learners: Diverger, Assimilator, Converger, and Accommodator. Each of these types combines two of the following approaches to learning--feeling, watching, thinking, and doing. These terms are contrasting yet associated, as this diagram suggests:

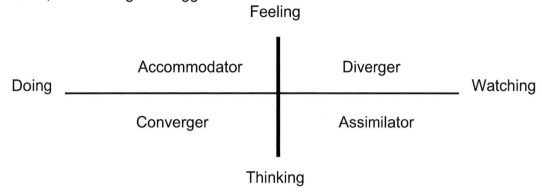

1. Diverger--Uses the processes of Feeling and Watching. These learners interpret the world mostly through feelings. They use tangible, perceiving tactics that are present-oriented, and rely on intuition. They learn by listening and sharing ideas. They succeed by watching an expert, or by modeling themselves after an authority. They like to hold back and reflect on a situation before taking action. They are creative and see many perspectives. They generate ideas, and are good at "brainstorming". They tend to be more emotional and interested in people. They learn best with games, role-playing, feedback, and discussions in a classroom. They see the teacher as a coach or helper.

2. Assimilator--Uses the processes of Watching and Thinking. These learners succeed by watching an expert and modeling themselves after an authority. They like to hold back and reflect on a situation before taking action. They prefer to think their way through a situation. They analyze and systematically plan things through; they use logic. They like to make, and analyze theories, and use inductive reasoning to put parts together for an explanation. They enjoy lectures, objective tests, textbooks, theory, traditional classrooms and play an observer role in learning. They see the teacher as a guide or task-master.

3. Converger--Uses the processes of Thinking and Doing. These learners use logic, but want knowledge to "do" something. This ability centers on doing or applying knowledge directly. Their learning comes from trial-and-error approaches and activity. They take risks. They use deductive reasoning. They are relatively unemotional and prefer to deal with things rather than people. They are very practical problem-solvers. They do best with situations that have correct answers, using facts and data for strategic thinking. Good with intelligence tests. Enjoy reading, studying alone with well-structured information. They are best for independent learning options. See the teacher as the communicator of information.

4. Accommodator--Uses the processes of Doing and Feeling. They interpret the world mostly through feelings. They learn by listening and sharing ideas. They rely on intuition. They are interested in active learning; doing things, making things happen, carrying-out

plans. They are risk-takers and adaptable. They will alter plans or theories if they don't work. Rely on others for information rather than their own analytic ability. They are very people-oriented, but impatient. They usually jump into a situation before gathering all the information. They do well with non-traditional classroom formats, such as accelerated courses and experiential learning.

So, do any of these types of learners sound like you? Again, taking the Learning Style Inventory (LSI) will give you a more precise indication of your abilities and preferences. The LSI is based on the research of Kurt Lewin and Carl Jung and the personality typing of the Myers-Briggs Inventory. You may want to know more about these researchers and their work in order to gain a greater understanding of learning theory and you.

When beginning a course of study, it is helpful if you:

1. Select a major area of study which fits your personal and career goals, as well as your learning style--don't fight your abilities.

2. Select courses that fit your learning style. Enjoyment and success are big motivators towards any goal. Undoubtedly, there will be requirements for a degree program that are either less interesting or more difficult for you. You may want to take them later, as you progress and become more confident in your abilities. A word of caution - DO NOT WAIT UNTIL YOUR LAST SEMESTER TO TAKE THOSE COURSES YOU DISLIKE. The requirements will still be there and they will somehow grow larger and more intimidating if you wait until the very last moment to satisfy them. One of the writers, a former academic advisor, remembers more than one student who failed to graduate on time when those "scary" requirements--math or science courses, for instance--were put off until the end. All it takes is a course scheduling conflict, or an emergency life event to ruin graduation plans.

3. Select teaching methods that fit your learning style. Telecourses or home-study classes may seem more amenable to your lifestyle. However, you may need structure or interaction with other classmates in order to learn best. Choose instructional methods that enhance your learning.

College is more than adding up credits. It is your chance to LEARN.

CAREERS

ACCOMMODATOR
Management, Banking, Public Administration, Accountant, Marketing, Business, Retail, Politician, Public Relations, Government Administration, Sales

DIVERGER
Literature, Theater, Television, Journalism, Athlete, Psychology, Musician, Designer, Personnel, Social Work

CONVERGER
Economics, Farming, Mining, Forestry, Medicine, Computer Science, Physician, Med. Tech., Applied Scientist, Manager

ASSIMILATOR
Education, Ministry, Sociology, Law, Researcher, Financier, Biology, R&D, Professor, Mathematics

EXERCISE: Learning Styles

Research shows that you can increase your chances of learning by up to 50% if you set clear and meaningful learning goals. The exercise which follows will help you do this. It will also give you a chance to test and apply your understanding of the four-step experiential learning process. Use additional sheets of paper if you need more space.

Note: In Chapter Three you will learn how to earn credit via the Portfolio process. In addition to documenting your experiences for college credit, you will be required to write a paper describing the learning that occurred. Many schools use Kolb's model as the basis for the "life-learning" Portfolio credits.

Step 1. Experiences

List the events or circumstances which led to your decision to go back to school (Example: "My boss has been pressuring me." "I've always wanted to complete my Bachelor's degree." "I've gone as far as I can go in this company without a degree.").
Expand on your thoughts.

Step 2. Reflections

What was it about these events that influenced your thinking or feelings? What values were touched by those circumstances? How do others feel about your decision to return to college? (Example: "I value and enjoy my job and respect my boss' suggestions." "Most of my family members have their degrees.") Expand on your thoughts.

Step 3. Concepts

Based on your experiences, reflections, and information from others, what do you want to (or need to) learn in your courses in college? List two or three learning areas and set some priorities for yourself. These are your learning goals. (Examples: "My company needs employees with Business, Management and Computer Information Systems knowledge." "I love Psychology and Music classes.") Expand on your thoughts.

Step 4. Planned Experiments

Now plan specific things to do during your first course that will help you to learn (your plans may change as you get into the program, but this gives you a start). Refer to the description of your learning style for some ideas. (Examples: "I'll take an Introduction to Computers course and apply my learning to a project at work." "I'll study two hours every evening.") Expand on your thoughts.

Assessing Your Lifestyle

Establishing Priorities—

The Who, What, Where, When, And Why Of Time Management

Adult learners juggle many responsibilities at one time--family, jobs, and personal interests. You are probably no exception. Going back to school means hard work and requires a lot of study time. A commitment to completing your degree will challenge your time management skills and necessitate a careful look at your priorities. You will have to make decisions about your TIME and how you want to spend it. How can you fit in new learning? What will you let go? Can you count on support from your family and friends? Support from your manager at work?

 EXERCISE: Priorities

1.   List those activities that demand your time (children, job, spouse, extended family, hobbies, sports, volunteer work, housework, other responsibilities)

Example:

a. Full-time job
b. Playing tennis
c. Driving kids to school

d. _____

e. _____

f. _____

g. _____

h. _____

i. _____

j. _____

k. _____

2. Now, go back to your list and:

O = Circle the numbers of those activities which you CANNOT give up.
* = Put an asterisk by those activities which other people can do.
X = Cross out those activities which you can/will give up entirely.

Make sure to talk to the people who are affected by your decisions, as well as those who can provide you with help. If a high point of the week for you and your spouse is that weekly tennis date, consult with him/her before eliminating it. On the other hand, perhaps your boss will let you leave work early for a late afternoon class if you eat lunch at your desk.

Study time and good study habits are necessary for success. You'll need to establish YOUR quiet space and time for reading, writing assignments, and preparing for tests. Select a comfortable (yet not too comfy) chair and a well-lighted area with a desk for writing and typing. If you do not live alone, you'll have to work out study time "contracts" with your family, children and/or roommate to provide you with the time and atmosphere you need to study. One busy adult learner we know posts a Do Not Disturb sign outside of her study area. Her family knows that only in the case of serious emergencies should she be disturbed. You can also make use of study time in the car by listening to recorded lecture tapes, reading your assignments on your lunch breaks, or studying while riding the bus to work. You'll have to be creative to make sure you get the TIME you need to study. Each class will require its own amount of study time. Some courses will be "easier" or "harder" for you depending on your learning style, interests and abilities. Most professionals feel that for every hour you spend in class you should spend a minimum of two hours studying. Many people require 3 hours or more of study time for every hour spent in class.

Most community colleges and many four-year institutions offer courses in study skills, test taking, test anxiety, and coping strategies for returning students. We strongly recommend that you take advantage of any or all of these courses. Beyond improving your skill in a particular area, you will meet other adult learners whose lives and challenges are similar to yours. You can create, or join "study buddy" groups for support.

Let's look at the resources adult learners have to succeed. Resources for support can be found in your home, your close circle of friends and family, your campus, and within yourself. Adult learners bring much more to the classroom than they think:

- More experiences from their careers and life in general
- Eagerness to learn
- Intensive commitment to complete their degree
- Focused use of their time
- Willingness to question material for a deeper understanding
- Higher expectations for good teachers
- Better sense of their goals

- A consumer orientation to their education
- Ability to prioritize and juggle multiple tasks
- Enhanced problem-solving skills

One of our clients is learning algebra--really learning it--this time around. She has a 12-year old daughter in an advanced math class. When her daughter gets stuck, now mom can help out. The first time around, the mother struggled and remained baffled by algebra, despite earlier excellent math grades. She is delighted to be able to assist her daughter. It has given her new confidence in her own academic skills. Like so many women a couple of generations ago, she developed a phobia for math. Now, her success feels wonderful! She attributes her new-found ability to years of problem-solving on both the domestic and work front, the ability to look at problems from many different perspectives, the flexibility she developed throughout life, and the confidence that maturity brings.

EXERCISE: Resource Checklist

Make a check mark by those resources which you have available, or could "tap" into from your community:

_____ Child Care	_____ Employer	_____ Computer
_____ Family Members	_____ Friends	_____ Study Skills Class
_____ Transportation	_____ Study Groups	_____ Campus Staff
_____ Libraries	_____ Study Time	_____ Spouse
_____ Assessments	_____ Tape Recorder	_____ Self-Motivation
_____ Television/VCR	_____ Adult Student Group	_____ Internet
_____ Grandchildren	_____ Room for study	_____ Other…

Assessing Your Financial Needs

Education is an investment!

"If you think education is expensive; try ignorance."
Dr. Derek Bok, Past-President, Harvard University

As you progress through this guidebook, you will have a better idea of the costs involved with earning your college degree. You'll decided on some colleges you plan to attend and the types of learning resources you plan to use. However, it is never too early to take time to do financial planning and to start researching sources for financial support.

There are basically two types of financial aid funding: 1) those which you have to pay back in the form of a loan 2) those which you do not have to pay back in the form of gifts such as grants or scholarships. Most financial aid is based upon your need in relation to the tuition of your college(s) of choice. Most campuses have financial aid advisors who can help you locate resources and assist you with any forms you will need to complete.

Unfortunately, Federal Funding and Financial Aid are very limited for the adult student. These sources give funds based on need. Because adults often have jobs, houses, investments and other assets, they are not considered. The government does afford for low – very low – interest rates on student loans. Check with your local bank for information.

A word of caution: There have been reports of scams involving companies that guarantee they will find you financial aid or scholarships. They charge a fee for their services and at best just send a list of some financial aid opportunities. These same opportunities can be found in directories at libraries and by doing "searches" on the Internet. One student actually missed out on financial aid because the information from one of these companies arrived after the deadline for many types of assistance.

The following organizations are well worth your time to research:

1. Federal Government--Pell Grants, Supplemental-Educational Opportunity Grant (SEOG). Perkins Loans, Stafford Loans, and the PLUS Loans/Supplemental Loans for Students
2. State Grants-In-Aid
3. College Work-Study Programs
4. Veterans Administration
5. Local City and County Scholarships
6. Scholarship Directories (local libraries), www.supercollege.com
7. Tuition Assistance Plans Provided by Employers
8. Banks
9. Private Funding – family, friends

Most college campuses will take major credit cards for tuition and books...

Appropriate educational expenses may be tax deductible....

First, you will want to chart your personal assets and liabilities to get a concrete and realistic view of your financial situation. Maybe a stricter budget for a few years is all you will need to sacrifice to complete your degree and pay for your college credits. However, after you review your financial status, you may have to find other means to generate the money you will need to pay for your education.

Here are a few tips to help you get your educational finances in order and to keep your educational expenses to a minimum:

1.   Make sure you plan well in advance. Financial aid is awarded for year round - Fall, Winter, and Spring/Summer terms. Financial aid offices become very busy just before the beginning of each academic term.

2.   Financial aid paperwork is very time-consuming and complex. Allow enough to complete the forms and wait for a response.

3.   If possible, make an appointment with a financial aid advisor months in advance to actually needing the funds for course registration. Come to the appointment well prepared. Have your questions written out in advance and all relevant papers (tax reports, bank statements, investment reports, others) readily available for examination.

4.   Utilize some the lower cost options (CLEP and portfolio, others - see Chapter 3) for gaining college credit to save time and money.

Notes:

EXERCISE: Charting Your Personal Finances

Expenses: Per Month Per Year

Rent/Mortgage   _____ _____
Utilities   _____ _____
Food   _____ _____
Telephone   _____ _____
Medical   _____ _____
Insurance   _____ _____
Child Care   _____ _____
Clothes   _____ _____
Transportation   _____ _____
Personal   _____ _____
Supplies   _____ _____
Credit Cards   _____ _____
Other Expenses   _____ _____
Other Debts   _____ _____

Education: Per Month Per Year
  Tuition   _____ _____
   Books   _____ _____
  Testing   _____ _____
  Portfolio   _____ _____
  Materials   _____ _____
  Travel Expenses   _____ _____

Resources:

Income   _____ _____
Savings   _____ _____
Nontaxable Income   _____ _____
Child Support/Alimony _____ _____
Investments   _____ _____
Other   _____ _____

Notes:

Questions For A College Academic Advisor Or Admissions Counselor

1. Do you offer the Learning Style Inventory (LSI) developed by Dr. David Kolb?

2. What program(s) of study seem to "fit" best with my learning style at present?

3. What program(s) of study seem to best utilize the credits I have already accrued?

4. Where might I find career counseling or courses that address career concerns?

5. What books do you recommend to help me understand career opportunities, personality characteristics, and learning styles? Are these available in the campus library?

6. Is it possible to earn a degree taking course work only at night or on weekends, or do some courses or programs of study require daytime attendance?

7. Is academic advising available after 5:00 p.m. and/or on weekends? What about other campus services?

8. Do you have a center for adult learners or special programs and services for adult learners? Is childcare available, especially evenings and weekends?

9. What type of Financial Aid does your school provide? Is the Financial Aid Office open after 5:00 p.m. or on weekends?

Take Time To Do Your Planning -- Right

CHAPTER TWO - SHOPPING FOR A COLLEGE

Choosing Your Major ....

should be more than a shot in the dark!

"I'm forty-one years old and need to advance my career, but I'm unsure if I should stay with my present career track or consider which new career might be better for me. How do I decide on a college major?"

Most adults go to college to help them advance in their career or to change to a more lucrative or satisfying field. If you are unsure of your career direction, start with some career planning. Any library or bookstore will have a selection of books, tapes or videos on the subject. (Check the Reading Resources Directory at the end of this book for suggested titles). Sign up for a career-planning course at your local community college or adult education center. Private career counseling services cost more, but may give you more personal attention. As we mentioned in Chapter One, there are numerous inventories (not tests!) that are used in conjunction with career advising and can help you make an informed decision. Don't forget to inquire if your employer provides career services.

All degree programs require that you select a "major" area of study, such as Business, Secondary Education, Biology, Fine Arts. The Major defines which Department within the College or University you will utilize for most of your courses.

Once you have a better idea of what you want to be "when you grow up", find some people who already have that job and ask about their education. Don't be surprised if their degree Major doesn't match to their jobs. In many companies and professional positions, the fact that you have a college degree is more important than the subject of your studies. Other corporations seek specific requirements and related fields of study.

Remember what we said earlier - think like a consumer.

As you go through this process--yes, it *is* a process--you need to ask yourself a couple of important questions:

1.   Do I want to move up within my current organization?

or

2.   Do I want to change employment?

If you plan to stay with your current employer it is essential to talk to your supervisor, human resource office, or with someone who already has the type of job you hope to obtain. They can help you define what types of credentials are needed for that job. If you plan to apply with a different employer, you need to talk to their human resources professionals to make sure you know what educational background is required.

Consider - If you change employers, what will happen to your pension? Benefits? Income? As more and more employers hire temporary or contract workers, pensions and other employee benefits are not the entitlement they once were.

One professional we advised chose to stay with her current employer - a large telecommunications corporation - because she is "vested" and receives very good benefits – including Tuition Assistance. She works part-time (50%) to maintain benefits, while in her spare time is developing new skills to point her towards her next career with the same company.

A very popular "generalists" major is Business Administration or Business Management. Recently, enrollments have decreased in many schools of business because the market is becoming glutted with newly minted business school graduates. This does not mean these degrees do not have value – they do.

Technological fields (computers, telecommunications, etc.) of study require a very specific type of education. For example, the curriculum for a Computer Science degree is heavily based in mathematics and programming. A Computer Information Systems or Operations Management degree focuses on systems analysis and software applications. Majors often have "prescriptive" curricula – not much choice in course selection - when they are associated with precise expertise.

Similarly, a Master's of Business Administration (MBA) may focus too heavily on accounting and finance if you are a "people person", while a Master's of Arts (MA) in Human Resource Management may suit your career objectives better.

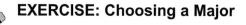 **EXERCISE: Choosing a Major**

Contact three companies to find out the "preferred" degree required for your target job.

Company	Job Title	Min. Degree & Major Required	Pref. Degree
AT&T	Product Dev.	BA/BS/MA in production mgt.	MA/prod. mgt.

1.
2.
3.

If you can quit your job, sell your house, and leave your family, you can still go to college the "traditional" way. Otherwise, you must find programs fit your life circumstances and are accessible to you.

 EXERCISE: Learning Providers

1. Start with the telephone directory and look for the "Colleges and Universities" category in the yellow pages. The number of listings will probably surprise you.

2. You will probably find a state university and several private colleges. You may know about your local community college and have seen the TV ads for local technical institutes. But what do you do about all those other listings? You must investigate all of them – you don't want to overlook an institution that may have the program you need.

Obviously, if you want a bachelor's degree in business administration, The Academy of Floral Design probably won't help. On the other hand, don't eliminate religious affiliated or more Liberal Arts colleges without finding out exactly what they have to offer. Using the system for earning college credits described in this book, you may end up using half a dozen institutions.

Hint: Always check with the institution you plan to graduate from regarding their specific policies about transfer credit. You don't want to take courses at one college/university that will not be accepted by your degree-granting institution.

One traditional university student we know decided to fulfill her foreign language requirement over the summer by taking courses at a community college in her home town. Imagine her dismay when she discovered she needed _prior approval_ to take a course off-campus. In her case, it took a lot of extra paper work to finally have the credits accepted.

On the other hand, you do not have to take all of your courses from the school where you plan to complete your degree. It is to your advantage to network options for credit and learning. This may save you time and money. Just remember to request approval in advance, and get the approval in writing before transferring credit. (Chapter 5 discusses using several colleges and options to complete your degree)

Accreditation

Most people think that accreditation is a simple proposition--a college is either accredited or it isn't. Unfortunately, it is not that easy. The U.S. Department of Education serves as the umbrella organization over about 80 different accrediting agencies. All schools of learning must also be accredited by the state(s) in which they operate.

Any, and all schools of learning that you contact will answer "Yes" to the question, "Are you accredited?" You must also find out which agency accredits them to be certain you are "buying" the education you want.

Recently, a young man came to us with the following problem:

"A few years ago, I attended a private/proprietary business college and earned an associate degree in computer science. At the time, I was told that this was an accredited program--and I landed a good job because of it. Now I want to finish my bachelor's degree, but the colleges I contacted will not transfer my credits because they are "unaccredited". I don't understand."

We informed him that his business "college" was accredited by the Accrediting Council for Independent Colleges and Schools (ACICS). The four-year institutions of higher education that he had contacted were all accredited by the North Central Association of Colleges and Schools (one of six regional accrediting agencies in the U.S. – see Resource Directory). Both are valid agencies, although they accredit very different kinds of learning--training vs. education. Regional Accreditation is the recognized council for accrediting higher education institutions. AICS accrediting boards tend to review vocational or training schools. Very few colleges will directly transfer credit from an ACICS school to any Regionally Accredited college/university.

Colleges accredited by the same agency usually recognize one another's credits. Luckily, we found a four-year college that belonged to both agencies and it accepted his previous business college credits, allowing him to earn a Regionally Accredited bachelor's degree.

When you think of a college or university, such as the University of Arizona, Harvard, Stanford, Colorado State University, Boston College – these all have Regional Accreditation. This status relates to the entire college or university.

There are also organizations that accredit – give a professional status to - specific programs/departments within a college or university. These additional stamps of approval are called Professional Accreditations. For example, many Business departments are additionally accredited by the American Assembly of Collegiate Schools of Business (AACSB), nursing programs by the National League for Nursing (NLN), teaching programs through the National Council for Accreditation of Teacher Education (NCATE) and engineering programs through the Accreditation Board for Engineering and Technology

(ABET). There are other departmental professional accrediting bureaus, but this gives you the idea.

This type of Professional accreditation is separate from, and/or in addition to, the institutional accreditation described earlier. If you expect to pursue a graduate degree in a professional area, this type of accreditation may be required of your undergraduate degree for competitive admission to a specific graduate program.

Some of the more known programs in first-rate schools are not professionally accredited, so don't get too hung up on the issue of specific program accreditation. Some schools find the criteria for accreditation to be at odds with the goals of their program and thus choose not to seek such accreditation. These accreditations are often very "traditional" in their requirements, and may not be fitting for an adult learner program.

The only way to be sure you are buying the education you need is to ask the school. If you are planning to transfer credit, or apply to a Graduate School program – work backwards when designing your education plan. Check the requirements for the highest level of study you will ever obtain, and make sure all the education you "buy" will fulfill their requirements as you move along in your studies. This will reduce your risk of being less competitive for admission to an undergraduate transfer program, or Graduate School.

Undergraduate Admissions

When selecting a college to attend, it is vital to research entrance qualifications. There are two tests that may be used for acceptance to an undergraduate program. They are the American College Testing (ACT) or the Scholastic Aptitude Test (SAT). Each college determines which test it will accept. Colleges may want to review your past academic performance on your "permanent record" from you high school--yes, that far back if necessary! -- and your test score on the admission exam. Admission exams often give unreliable information in predicting how an adult learner will perform in college since many life changes, and hopefully a good deal of maturation, have taken place since high school.

Because admissions exams are often not the best measurement of ability for adults, fewer adult learner programs are requiring them. Instead, they look at a variety of factors, including prior college grades, current or recent employment, a personal essay describing your educational background, employment history, and other relevant factors including educational and life goals.

Depending on the college that interests you, it may be necessary to begin your college work at an "open-admission" campus, such as a community college. These colleges allow most any student to enroll in programs – they give you the change to succeed. Therefore, they don't require any ACT or SAT exam. So, if you take about 12-18 credits of transferable academic coursework and apply to the 4-year college you want to attend – you are considered a "transfer" student. Thus, you've avoided taking any entrance admission exams for your undergraduate degree!

Pretty smart – eh?

Semesters And Quarters

Most colleges or universities operate on either a semester or quarter system.

A traditional semester lasts about 15-16 weeks and Fall semester usually begins in late August or early September, and ends in December. Spring semester begins in January and ends in May/June. Summer semester is often shorter in length. Usually, summer classes are fewer in number, but longer in time "periods" per class to fulfill the same amount of required "in the class" time.

The advantage of the semester system is that it includes a longer winter vacation with more in-depth analysis of course material.

Quarters last about 10 weeks with Fall quarter beginning in September and ending in mid-December. Winter quarter begins in January and ends in mid-March. Spring quarter runs from early April through mid-June. Schools operating on a quarter system usually offer a full-term summer quarter.

Advantages of the quarter system include less material to study for final exams, and more frequent breaks. Another advantage or a disadvantage (depends on how you view it) is that more courses are necessary to achieve the total credits required for graduation. This gives you the opportunity to take more classes of interest.

Colleges use a simple mathematical formula to convert credits from one system to the other for transfer purposes. One semester credit = 2/3 of a quarter credit. To determine the equivalent semester credits for 12 quarter credits, multiply by 2/3:

$$12 \text{ Quarter Hours} \times 2/3 = 8 \text{ Semester Hours}$$
$$8 \text{ Semester Hours} \times 3/2 = 12 \text{ Quarter Hours}$$

Students frequently complain that they lose credits when transferring from quarters to semesters, but that is really not the case; you just need more quarter hours to complete your degree. On the semester system you will need approximately 120 credits for a bachelor's degree, compared to about 180 credits on the quarter system.

Grades

Research has proven that adult learners earn better overall grades than do younger, traditional students. Adult learners are serious about their learning and education. They are not in college to "party" from their newfound freedom. They are there to learn. However, worrying about obtaining a perfect straight "A" transcript can reduce the enjoyment of learning. In order to stay in college, you must maintain a certain Grade Point Average (GPA) set by each institution. You can determine your GPA by the following formula:

A = 4 points, B= 3 points, C= 2 points, D= 1 point, F= 0 points

Multiply the number of points you earned by the number of hours of credits you have earned for each class and divide this figure by the total number of credit hours.

Example:	Course	Credit Hours	Grade	Honor Points
	Math 105	4	B (3.0)	12.0
	History 111	3	C (2.0)	6.0
	English 105	3	A (4.0)	12.0
	Psychology 171	3	B (3.0)	9.0
	TOTAL:	13		39.0

39 ÷ 13 = 3.0 = B average

As you can see, the grades are "weighted" by the number of credit hours. Thus, a B in a four-credit course is more heavily weighted than a B in a three-credit course. The weighting is important. One of the writers remembers her first term in college. She earned one A, two B's, and one C. She thought she had earned a straight B average. Unfortunately, the C was in a four-hour course and the remaining courses were all three credits. This gave her less than a 3.0 average. It was time to "hit the books" – and she did.

This same formula is used by most institutions. Colleges may assign different numerical coordinates and/or differentiate between plus and minus grades. For instance, an A might be worth 4 points and an A- 3.7 points. Some schools use only numerical grades, such as 3.0, which would correspond to a letter grade of B. Still other institutions use a numerical scale based on 100 points, where an A might be 90-100, a B would be 80-90, etc. As we have said before, check with a college official if the institution's policy is unclear to you. Never hesitate to ask a question. You can pretty much figure that if you have a question regarding a policy or procedure someone else has asked it before!

Now that you know something about grading systems, you need to know that most schools transfer grades and credits from other institutions, while others will transfer only credits.

Depending on your prior academic record - that can be good news or bad news. However, all your grades usually are used to evaluate for admission purposes.

Policies for repeating a course also differ from campus to campus. Some institutions average the grades, while others take only the most recently earned grade. When in doubt, ASK!

Sometimes adults who return to college have had poor grades from their previous college experience. If previous grades prevent you from meeting the admissions requirements of the college you now wish to attend, there are assorted strategies you may be able to employ in order to be admitted to your school of choice. First, you may repeat the course(s) in which you did poorly and do better. Even if grades are averaged and not replaced, as mentioned above, you are proving you are capable of doing the work. Second, you may take additional courses at an open admission college, such as a community college. These campuses allow anyone to enter with a high school diploma or appropriate scores on a General Education Diploma (GED) exam for high school equivalency. Additional higher grades earned at a Community College will raise your overall GPA and prove your ability and desire to succeed. Finally, you can see if the institution you plan to attend has an "academic forgiveness" policy. Academic forgiveness has become more and more available as adult learners return to college campuses. Although academic forgiveness policies vary in name and specific rules, normally previously earned poor grades remain on the transcript, but your GPA is given a fresh start.

Questions To Ask the College Academic Advisor or Admissions Counselor -

1. What type of accreditation does your campus have? Regional accreditation? Vocational accreditation? Professional/Departmental accreditations?

2. What classes will your campus take in transfer? How many credits will transfer?

3. Does your campus operate on a quarter or semester system? How are credits converted from one system to the other?

4. Is an entrance exam required for your selected degree program (Associate or Bachelor)?

5. Does the institution have an academic forgiveness policy?

6. Are grades transferred or just credits?

7. How are repeat grades handled?

8. What affect will the answers to questions 5, 6, and 7 have on my admission and permanent record (transcript) at this institution?

Now, complete the following information for <u>each</u> college in your area that you are considering attending. Define your major area of study for each campus. Record admissions tests that are required and find out if those exams are absolutely necessary for an adult student.

College/University _____

Major_____ Accreditation(s)_____

Admissions Test Required_____Semester_____ Quarter_____

Transferability of Credits: Grade Required_____

Maximum Number of Credits Taken in Transfer from two-year schools _____

Maximum Number of Credits Taken in Transfer from four-year schools _____

Transfer Credit

Every college or university has its own policy on transferring credits from other institutions. There are no universal or nationally accepted transfer policies. If you want to take a course at College A and transfer the credits to College B, you must check with College B about transferability before you take the course at College A! It wouldn't hurt to get the answer in writing, and while you're at it, find out how the course will fit into your total degree program.

Grades for Transfer

Many colleges will only transfer courses for which the student earned an A, B, or C grade. Some colleges will accept all Pass (P) grades and some will accept a very minimal amount of earned D grades. Courses that were failed (F) or not completed (Incomplete, Withdrew) will not transfer.

Course Content for Transfer

Colleges/universities will often only accept through transfer those courses that have content similar to what the receiving institution offers. If, for example, you took Astronomy 101 at University X, but Urban College Y does not offer a similar course, the credits may not transfer.
Course content will also determine how (or if) the credit will count toward your degree. A course categorized as Humanities at one college may be Social Science credit at another college. Also, many community colleges grant credit for vocational subjects, such as electronics, drafting or secretarial science. Often, these "Applied" subject credits are more difficult to transfer to most four-year colleges and universities.

Age of Credits

Some colleges place an age limit on transfer credits and will only accept credits earned within the last five or ten years. Luckily for adults returning to complete a degree, most colleges have eliminated the age limit on credits in all but the more technical subjects. Thus, the curriculum for French 101 has stayed relatively constant through the years, whereas courses in Computer Science change drastically every few years. Courses that have curriculum "longevity" are "safer" to transfer than those courses which are continually being updated.

Graduate degree programs are more likely to enforce limits on the age of credits.

Number of Credits

Most undergraduate degrees require about 120.0 (semester) credits of study, in specified fields, for graduation. There is usually a maximum number of credits which an institution will accept in transfer. Likewise, there is a minimum number of credits which must be earned directly from the degree-granting institution. This is sometimes referred to as a "residency requirement" and is usually equal to about one year's worth of college work, or 30.0 credits for a bachelor's degree. So, if you earned 105.0 credits at a four-year college, usually a maximum of 90.0 credits would be considered for transfer to another college or university. Many institutions distinguish between credits earned at four-year institutions vs. two-year institutions. Community Colleges offer 2-year, or Associate degrees equaling 60.0 credits. Thus, most 4-year institutions will not accept more than 60.0 credits from community colleges. So, don't take more than 60.0 credits at any community college.

Upon earning 60.0 credits, you need to transfer to a 4-year college/university or you will lose time and money trying to complete a Bachelor's degree.

Non-Traditional Credits

Some colleges and universities do not recognize credits earned through various "non-traditional methods, such as correspondence, telecourses, tests or assessment of prior learning (see chapters 3 and 4). This is a clue that these schools may be too "traditional" and not understanding of the needs of the adult student. As a matter of fact, some college/universities say point blank that they don't want adult learners – their mission is to service only the "traditional" young college students.
When in doubt about a college policy, always check with their academic advisor.

Degree Completion Programs

Some colleges/universities offer every course needed to complete at degree at their institution. Some programs, designed specifically for adult students, may offer courses for the Junior or Senior year of study – only the upper-level courses to complete the degree at their institution. This means you have to come to their school with half your degree already completed - or 60.0 transferable credits. Most often, these colleges will refer you to a local community college to gain those lower-level courses that will fulfill their requirements. Once you complete your first 60.0 credits, then you can apply to the 4-year, degree-completion program and finish your Bachelor's degree. These programs are very common, because they are less expensive for colleges to design since they don't have to offer all courses at night, weekend or accelerated – just those courses to complete your major and other upper-level requirements.

   **Notes About This Chapter:**

CHAPTER THREE –
EARN COLLEGE CREDIT FOR WHAT YOU KNOW

Give Yourself Some Credit!

"I've been using computers on the job for ten years, do I have to take an introductory computer course?"

"I taught cultural diversity in the military. Does that count for anything?"

"My employer offers numerous in-house sales training courses. In the twelve years I've been with the company, I've attended at least one or two workshops a year. They were just as hard as my college classes. Will they apply toward my degree?"

"I've read everything there is to read about the Civil War and visited the sites of most of the major battles. On weekends I sometimes participate in battle re-enactments. Can I get some history credit for this?"

Most learning occurs outside the classroom. Think about it. Where did you learn most of what you know about doing your job? About being a good parent? Handling your finances?

If you're like most people, you learned these things by *doing* them. You probably picked up additional information through some of the following methods:

- Reading books, magazines and newspapers
- Asking questions
- Talking to experts
- Watching and mimicking people who know how to
- Trial and error
- Following written instructions
- Relating the current situation to similar events
- Watching an instructional video
- Searching for help online

All of these experiences can lead to legitimate learning. Some colleges and universities are "open" to the fact that even when you are not sitting in a college classroom, you might be learning something equal to the same content in their courses. These schools have devised different methods to evaluate learning for college credit.

"Credit For Prior Learning" (also called *experiential learning*) is becoming a more accepted practice as adults make up a large proportion of college students. There are more than 1200 colleges and universities which offer methods to grant some form of this credit. Remember, it is not just an "experience" that will award you college credit – but the ability to demonstrate you gained college equivalent knowledge.

Here are the most recognized options:

- •Military training
- •Corporate training
- •Professional certification, Licenses
- •Testing
- •Portfolio

Remember, not all schools grant credit for prior learning. You must check with the college where you plan to complete your degree about their policies. The opportunity to earn credit for what you already know can greatly reduce the amount of *TIME* you spend in completing your degree and reduce the *COST*!

The adult learner comes to higher education with an acquired level of learning in many college equivalent areas of study. Below we describe the major methods used to assess and award college credit for subject areas in which you may already have acquired a college level of expertise.

Ace Credit

The American Council on Education (ACE) uses teams of college faculty to evaluate thousands of standard, formal training courses, offered by organizations such as the branches of military service, major corporations and professional associations. Their recommendations for equivalent college credit are published in reference books that are the size of big telephone books.

We'll start with ACE guidelines for military training. If you were never in the military, skip ahead to learn about corporate training.

Military Training

Everyone who has been in the military for at least six months has received some training that may be used for college credit. How do we know? Because the first thing everybody in the military takes is Basic Training, and most colleges and universities grant physical education credit for Basic Training. Isn't that great? You may already own college credit and not know it! It doesn't stop with Basic Training, there are many courses from military training that are worth college credit.

ACE has evaluated and recommends college credit for approximately 30% of all training courses offered to military personnel. *The Guide To The Evaluation of Educational Experiences in the Armed Services* gives a detailed analysis of these courses. Military occupational specialty (MOS) numbers and Navy enlisted ratings are designations evaluated for credit. These volumes represent all branches of the military, and date back to the 1940's. You can find these directories at most colleges/universities, or research online at: **www.acenet.edu**.

Your discharge papers (DD 214), or duty and training papers if you're still active, provide the official transcript of your military training. If the information on your DD 214 matches the ACE criteria to receive credit and your chosen college adheres to the ACE "recommendations", they award credit on your college transcript. This can be trickier than it sounds. First, *all* the criteria listed must match. This includes location of training, date of course, and course number.

Let's say you took a course at Fort Meade that sounds just like the one described in the ACE guide, except the location indicated in the guidebook is Fort Sumter. You won't receive direct college credit. The same is true if the dates don't match. If the guidebook indicates the course started August 1, 1986, but you took it in 1985 – no credit. *Everything must match.*

Second, the credits recommended must not duplicate college courses you've already taken. For example, look at the credit recommendation for the Non-Commissioned Officer's school (NCO) course listed below. According to ACE, this course is equivalent to a course in Principles of Management. If you've already taken a college course in principles of management, the college will not grant you additional credits for the same course taken through your ACE military training.

Third, the recommended credits must apply to your chosen major and degree. For example, if you are studying for a degree in History, Principles of Management would not be a required course. At best, it might be classified as an elective. However, if you've already fulfilled your requirement for electives, then this ACE course is not useful. Credits earned through ACE recommendations must fit into college's regular degree program requirements.

The good news is that students usually don't have to pay any fees to have ACE/Military credits put on their transcripts. Free credit! Who can afford to pass that up?

You can obtain a listing of your ACE military courses from you branch of the military.

Now, look at these examples of course evaluations from the ACE guide for military training:

1. Army - Supply (SU-CMF) Noncommissioned Officer (NCO) Basic, AR-1408-0044
   Course Number: 5 -SU-C40A.
   Location: Quartermaster School, Ft. Lee, Virginia
   Length: 10-12 weeks (353-420 hours).
   Exhibit Dates: 3/73-6/85
   Objectives: To train enlisted personnel to perform as noncommissioned officers in supply.
   Instruction: Lectures and practical exercises in the function of noncommissioned officers in supply, including leadership, logistical combat support, maintenance management, communicative techniques, introduction to career management field, DSU accounting procedures, mechanized stock control procedures at DSU level, ASDA accounting procedures for repair parts, storage of repair parts, special accounting procedures, and ASDA accounting procedures.
   Credit Recommendations: In the vocational certificate category, 3 semester hours in principles of management (7/74); in the lower-division baccalaureate/associate degree category, 3 semester hours in principles of management (7/74); in the upper-division baccalaureate category, 3 semester hours in principles of management (7/74).

2. Navy - Intercultural Relations - Facilitator Training, NV-1512-0003
   Course Number: A-SK-0011
   Location: Naval Amphibious School, San Diego, California
   Length: 18 weeks (720 hours).
   Exhibit Dates: 7/72-1/88.
   Objectives: To train enlisted personnel to facilitate intercultural relations programs.
   Instruction: Lectures and practical exercises in intercultural programs. Course includes leadership skills, team building processes, cultural awareness, course familiarization, communications skills, dynamics of change, and supervised teaching.
   Credit Recommendation: In the lower-division baccalaureate/associate degree category, 3 semester hours in human relations or basic psychology. In the upper-division baccalaureate category, 3 semester hours in group dynamics, and, on the basis of institutional evaluation, 6 in supervised teaching (8/74).

As you can see, credit can be awarded for many different courses – Psychology, Teaching, Management, Group Dynamics. Lots of military training is devoted to more "technical" courses – Radar, Electronics, Equipment use. These courses may also be acceptable to many colleges, and classified as "General Elective" credit

If you served in the Air Force, your training may be documented through the Community College of the Air Force (CCAF) - a regionally accredited institution in its own right. Request a copy of your transcript by writing to:

Registrar's Office
Community College of the Air Force
130 West Maxwell Road
Maxwell Air Force Base, AL 36112-6613
www.au.af.mil/ar/ccaf

Transcript requests must include your complete name (and maiden name), Social Security number, signature and current address with your zip code. There is no charge for CCAF transcripts.

EXERCISES: ACE Military Credit

To complete these exercises, you need to have made some preliminary choices about the academic major you want to pursue and the college(s) you want to consider.

Materials needed:

DD 214 or CCAF transcripts
Catalog from your college(s) of choice
The Guide to the Evaluation of Educational Experiences in the Armed Services or go to:
www.militaryguides.acenet.edu

1. Check your DD 214 for accuracy. Is all of your military training listed? If not, contact your local military office for information on how to obtain your military training records. It may well be worth your effort!

2. Look in the catalog index under "military training" or use the internet/online search for your military training course(s). The college may have a standard policy for granting credit for basic training or other military courses.

3. If the college accepts ACE military credit, take your training record to a college academic advisor and have them review your military experience for college credit.

4. Check every training course or occupational code listed on your training record against the information in the guidebook. *Remember, everything has to match.* Write down the credit recommendations for every course, including basic training.

5. Finally, examine the college catalog for your degree requirements and note where you think your military training will apply. Always check with a counselor or academic advisor to make sure your work is accurate.

6. Keep all this information together in a file folder labeled, "Military Training."

Don't despair if you fail to find your training courses in the ACE Guide. Remember, only about 30% of military courses have been evaluated. Make a list of your training that is not evaluated. We'll get back to this list later.

Corporate Training

Many large corporations offer a wide variety of in-house training courses for their employees. Just like with military training, the American Council on Education (ACE) has evaluated hundreds of such courses for equivalent college credit. You can find their recommendations in *The National Guide to Educational Credit for Training Programs*. For more information go to: **www.acenet.edu** and click-on "College Credit Recommendation Center" on the left-side menu bar.

The guidebook, or internet site contains information on other non-collegiate educational programs from:

- Large corporations
- Professional associations
- Labor unions
- Government agencies and departments

If you meet all the criteria of your ACE training course, your college may award ACE credits toward completing your degree. How do you meet the criteria? All you have to do is present a certificate of completion to your college. ALL the criteria listed in the course description (see examples below) must match. This includes location, date of course, and course number. Make sure any ACE Corporate credits will apply to your degree requirements. Usually, there is no additional cost to put ACE credits on your transcript.

Take a look at these example courses from the *ACE Guide*:

1. AT&T - Center for Systems Education. Data Gathering for System Development
   Course Number: IE2510
   Location: Piscataway, NJ and other AT&T locations.
   Length: 24 hours (4 days)
   Dates: October 1983- Present
   Objectives: To cover data gathering plans, interviewing techniques, questionnaire design, content analysis, observation, and paperwork flow.
   Instruction: In addition to lectures and discussion, students practice data gathering techniques in group exercises and role plays. Upon completion of this course, the student should be able to: (1) plan and organize a data collection project; (2) discuss the advantages and disadvantages of the five major data collection techniques; (3) design, construct, and evaluate a questionnaire; and (4) plan, conduct, and record an interview.

Credit Recommendation: In the upper division baccalaureate category, 1 semester hour in Business Administration, Computer Science, or Computer Information Systems (7/85).

2. National Association of Realtors. Quantitative Methods
    Course Number: EX 10
    Location: At various locations throughout the U.S. and Canada.
    Length: 30 hours (1 week)
    Dates: October 1973- Present
    Objective: To provide the participants with an understanding of the role of market analysis in feasibility studies, along with the ability to analyze, interpret, and present the data relating to market studies.
    Instruction: Lecture, workshops, classroom exercises, and drill problems designed to acquaint the students with quantitative techniques and applications.
    Credit Recommendation: In the upper division baccalaureate category, 2 semester hours in Quantitative Methods (10/83).

As you can see, you can obtain college credits in many areas of study – Statistics, Business, Computer Science, and many other areas.

 EXERCISE: ACE Corporate Credit

Use the course descriptions above to answer this question.

Sarah R. took an AT&T course in Data Gathering for System Development in January of 1994. The course ran for five days, six hours per day, for a total of 30 hours. Does this course qualify for the recommended one semester hour?

Answer: No, the course description specifies a class that is 24 hours (4 days) in length. It doesn't matter that Sarah's course was *longer* than the one described. All criteria must match exactly.

Some other organizations included in the ACE/Corporate guide are:

- American Institute of Banking
- Bell Communications
- Certified Employee Benefit Specialist Program
- College for Financial Planning
- Federal Aviation Administration

- General Electric Company
- General Motors Corporation
- IBM
- NCR Corporation
- U.S. Postal Service
- Other government departments
- Westinghouse Electric Corporation
- Xerox Corporation
- Many others.

It is well worth your time and effort to investigate this ACE guidebook to see if you already own college credit! Most colleges charge no additional fees to have ACE/Corporate credits put on their transcripts towards your graduation requirements.

EXERCISE: ACE Corporate Credit

1. Go through your records and collect your certificates and other information about corporate or professional training you've taken. Contact your training or human resources department for a record of your training. Include seminars and conferences you've attended. Most large companies keep these records in a computer database and can easily print a copy for you.

2. Examine these records for accuracy and make a list of any training that is not listed.

3. Keep these records together in a file folder or manila envelope labeled, "Corporate and Professional Training."

Many corporations contract with local colleges and universities to evaluate specific training courses that are taken by most of their employee. These partnerships are not listed in any one directory. Check with each of your local institutions for any such arrangements with industry or consult a representative in your corporation's Human Resource/Education and Training department. Even if college has not already evaluated a training course for college credit, they might be able to do so per your request. These arrangements allow corporations to support adult learners and gain a cost-containment measure for the company's Tuition Assistance Plans (TAP). This process is also a great "marketing" tool for colleges, but that's OK if it helps you too. Be aware, that most college/universities that do their own evaluation of corporate training courses will only grant credit towards <u>their</u> degree programs – their evaluations most likely will not transfer to other institutions.

PONSI Credits

The Directory of National Programs On Noncollegiate Sponsored Instruction (PONSI) is similar to the ACE *Guides* described above. This *Directory* is published by The State University System of New York, which has evaluated hundreds of training programs given by many "closed" organizations. You must be a member of many of these organizations to be part of their training courses.

If you meet the criteria presented for these courses, you may receive college credit towards your degree. Usually students do not have to pay additional fees to have PONSI credits put on their transcript towards meeting graduation requirements. You can find the *Directory* at your local public library, a college library or counseling center.

For information, go to: **www.nationalpoinsi.org**

Here's an example course from the PONSI *Directory*:

New York City Police Department. Introduction To Law
    Location: Police Academy, 235 East 20th Street, New York, NY
    Length: Version 1: 62 hours
              Version 2: 63 hours (11 weeks)
    Dates: Version 1: January 1974 - May 1980
              Version 2: June 1980- Present
    Objectives: To provide the student with a basic introductory course in law with emphasis on the development of legal principles and concepts having application to law enforcement.
    Instruction: The nature of law in contemporary society; study of the U.S. Constitution with emphasis on the Bill of Rights and the Fourteenth Amendment; constitutional rights of the accused; the police officer and the judicial process; application of legal concepts (probable cause, stop and frisk); court testimony.
    Credit Recommendation: Version 1: In the lower division baccalaureate/associate degree category or in the upper division baccalaureate category, 4 semester hours in Criminology, Government, Police Science, or Political Science (8/74). Version 2: In the lower division baccalaureate/associate degree category or in the upper division baccalaureate category, 4 semester hours in Government, Police Science, or Political Science (4/85 revalidation).

Note the different areas of credit awarded – Government, Police Science, Political Science.

 EXERCISE: PONSI Credits

Materials needed:

Your file or envelope marked, "Corporate and Professional Training"
Previous college transcripts
Catalog from your college(s) of choice
PONSI Guide

1. Look in the college catalog index under "corporate training," or "PONSI." Read any indicated policies.

2. If the college accepts PONSI recommendations , take your training record to a college academic advisor to research for college credit, or do some investigating yourself by reviewing the PONSI guidebooks in your public library, a college library in your community, or online.

3. Check every training course listed on your training record against the information in the guidebook. *Remember, everything has to match.* Write down the credit recommendations for every training course you find through PONSI.

4. Finally, examine the college catalog for your degree requirements and note where you think your professional training will apply. Always check with a counselor or academic advisor to make sure your work is accurate.

Don't despair if you fail to find your training courses in the ACE *Guide* or the PONSI *Directory*. Keep a list of your training which is *not* evaluated. We'll get back to this list later.

Testing Programs

"I'm Hispanic and my family made sure I learned and spoke Spanish from my early childhood. Is there any way to earn college credit for my knowledge without taking a course in Spanish that I could probably teach?"

How do you feel about taking tests? If you have in-depth knowledge of a subject or if you enjoy studying on your own, you may be able to earn college credit by taking and passing tests. This is a good option for people who typically do well on multiple-choice, true/false or essay tests. There are several different types of testing options. One, or more of them, should be available on-site at your college or university.

EXERCISE: Credit by Exams

Check the index of your college catalog(s) for their policies on "credit by examination" options.

CLEP Exams

The College Level Examination Program (CLEP) is a national series of examinations designed by the College Board to validate college level learning in a wide range of subject areas. These tests are widely available and comparatively inexpensive. CLEP tests equate to freshman or sophomore level (lower division) credit. For more information, go to: **www.collegeboard.com** and click-on CLEP EXAMS.

Currently, the fee to take a CLEP test is about $40 and most colleges will grant 3-6 semester credits for each test. There are study guides available at many college bookstores or you can write to The College Board for their study and registration materials. CLEP is the nation's most widely accepted credit-by-examination program. Almost two-thirds of all colleges and universities grant credit for satisfactory scores on the CLEP examinations. However, every institution sets its own policy about which exams the college will accept, and passing scores. The types of examinations are listed below:

1. General Exams - Focus on broad areas of study and are at the level of courses you would take in your first or second years of study (Freshman or Sophomore years).
Topics include: English Composition, Humanities, Mathematics, Natural Sciences, and Social Sciences and History.

Several study guides are available covering the six CLEP general exams, including complete practice exams.

2. Subject Exams - The 30 subject area tests let you demonstrate the specific knowledge and skills you may have gained through job experience, outside course work, or specialized independent reading. These examinations require a higher degree of specialized knowledge and training. Topics include American Government, General Psychology, French, German, Spanish, American Literature, College Algebra, Computers and Data Processing, Introduction to Management, etc.

The College Board publishes a study guide covering all thirty subject exams. Visit a college bookstore or library for a copy of this book. While you're there, look at the textbooks for courses in your subject area. Reviewing a college textbook is an excellent way to study for a subject exam.

The Academic Advising Center of any local college should be able to tell you where you can take the tests, or contact CLEP for a listing of test sites.

Excelsior College Exams – Also known as PEP Exams

Another national examination program is offered by Excelsior College. This series of Proficiency Examination Programs (PEP) covers material comparable to one or two semester courses in the Arts and Sciences, Business, Education, and Nursing. These tests are longer, more expensive (about $50- $200), and less frequently offered than the

CLEP tests. However, many of the Excelsior tests will give you more credit per exam and can award upper-division or graduate credit. Check with your local college for specific policies regarding credits earned and satisfactory scores for these exams. Free information and study guides are available from Excelsior College. For more information, go to: **www.excelsior.edu** and click-on Exams.

Thomas Edison State College Exams – TECEP Exams

Thomas Edison State College offers more than 50 examinations that allow students to earn college credit without taking formal courses. These examinations, known as TECEP® tests, are specifically designed to permit students to demonstrate the college-level knowledge they have gained through work, personal interests, or independent study by taking a single examination.

Originally, the tests were only available to Thomas Edison State College students. Now TECEP® examinations are available to anyone who is interested in earning college credit-by-examination. Students at many other colleges and universities have found wide acceptability for TECEP® credit at their home institutions.

TECEP® examinations are available in a wide range of business and liberal arts subjects, such as psychology, management, English composition and marketing.

Each test has its own test description that includes an outline of test topics, textbooks, and sample questions. Using the test description, students can study at their own pace and register to take the exam when they feel they are ready. If a student registers for a TECEP® test and plans change, as happens with busy adults, the test can rescheduled for another date.

For more information, got to: **www.tesc.edu/students/tecep/tecep.php**

Placement Exams

Placement tests are exams given to determine a level of competency and are not necessarily designed to award college credit. They are given by colleges to determine your level of expertise in specific subject areas, such as Math and English. The scores you achieve on placement tests help your advisor determine which courses you are prepared to take. Some colleges require you to take placement tests prior to being admitted to certain courses - a good example are Foreign Language placement tests, designed to assess the level of a foreign language course for which you should enroll (i.e., Introduction, Intermediate or Advanced). Fees for these tests will vary. Sometimes these tests don't award college credit, but will give you a "waiver". This means you may test-out of a course, but you still need to take a substitute course to earn 3.0 credits. Make sure you consult with an academic advisor at a college to clarify this issue.

Challenge Exams

Many colleges provide their own tests go access equivalent knowledge to courses listed in their catalogs or bulletins. These are called challenge exams and may actually be the final examination given to students enrolled in the course. Usually, you may speak with a department chairperson or professor of a certain course in which you feel you already have competency. Study the text book and take the challenge exam for credit in the course. Fees for challenge exams vary. You may have to pay the same tuition rate as if you enrolled in the course, or their fees may be much less than the tuition. Even if taking challenge exams doesn't save you money, this alternative will save you time.

EXERCISE: Test Preparation

Take a trip to your favorite library or bookstore and locate books on test preparation. After reading some of that material, review the list of Excelsior Exams.

Do any of the subjects catch your eye?
Do you have knowledge in any of the subjects listed?

If so, read the description of that test. Excelsior can answer questions and give you information on the type of test, number and kind of questions and topics covered. They also have study materials, with sample questions, and tips on how to study for the exam.

Make a list of the tests you're interested in taking.

Portfolio Process

You have now looked at several standardized methods for converting "life learning" into college credit. Chances are good there are still more subjects you know well, but which didn't fit with the previous options. You may have gained this knowledge in many ways, including:

- Hobbies
- Job skills
- Clubs and organizations
- Recreational activities
- Leisure pursuits
- Life skills

The Portfolio Process is another way to earn college credit for what you already know. Usually this is done through the preparation and presentation of a formal "Portfolio". The contents of the portfolio will vary according to the specifications of the college. Many schools offer a course to help their students put together a portfolio. Portfolio requires a lot of writing, and advanced skills in this area. You actually create large binders with all your Portfolio information, and this binder is sent to an appropriate professor to evaluate for college credit.

You may earn credit in any area in which the college offers classroom credit. In order for colleges and universities to grant credit you must demonstrate the level and extent of the learning. Here's an example:

> You may have worked in a supervisory capacity in industry for ten years. Almost all colleges offer a course in Principles of Supervision/Management. With a background in management, you have probably learned the principles or "theory" through seminars and classes at work. You have also gained knowledge on the "practical" side from your experiences as a manager or supervisor.
>
> Your learning has been based on performing the job duties, working with people, attending short seminars and week-long training classes, reading books and professional journals, networking with other managers, and a little trial-and-error experiential learning.

If you can demonstrate that through your experiences you learned essentially the same things you would have learned if you took the college course, you will be granted credit. You demonstrate your knowledge by writing a lengthy essay (usually 10+ pages which includes the theory aspect of your subject), participating in an oral interview, demonstrating or giving a hands-on presentation of your competency. Documentation is also necessary to verify that you did in fact participate in the learning experiences which you describe.

EXERCISE: Portfolio Credit

1. Go through your college catalog and select course descriptions that match your knowledge areas. By now there should be quite a few things at which you excel, and may be even an expert. You can select areas centered on your work and career development, skills you learned and use in your home, avocations, sports, and hobbies that you have perfected through the years (i.e., computer skills, accounting skills, playing tennis, gardening, raising a child who has MS or other disorders, painting, etc.). This is also where you can use the lists you compiled earlier of your training courses that were not evaluated by ACE or PONSI.

2. Make a master list of all the courses you identify.

3. Check the degree requirements listed in the catalog and eliminate any potential Portfolio credit for courses that do not fit into your program.
Some topics lend themselves best to a specific methodology. Knowledge of keyboards

(typing) can easily be demonstrated, but difficult to write an essay about. Competency in watercolor painting or song writing can best be evaluated by a presentation of your original works. On the other hand, it would be difficult to evaluate a parent's knowledge of child psychology by simply bringing your children to the instructor. This type of credit must have extensive theory and documentation to equal a college course.

Not all learning is equal to college credit. Tending a lawn and vegetable garden will not earn college credit for horticulture. But gardening accompanied by reading and study about soil, fertilizers, plant science, and landscaping design could be represented through an appropriately designed portfolio for college credit. Regular church attendance alone does not necessarily result in college level learning about religious philosophy. However, extensive reading of religious literature, customs and philosophy, attending conferences, and giving lectures may all be combined to demonstrate a college course in Religion and/or Philosophy.

Below is an example of a Portfolio presentation submitted by an adult student who was awarded college credit for her "life experiences". Note the different components of this student's writing and the *documentation* that was included to support her experiences. Forms of documentation can include letters from supervisors verifying your work, certificates of training, awards, newspaper or magazine articles. You can be very creative in documenting you abilities, such as taking photographs of your artwork or sculptures (you could even bring them to faculty the assessing your work), demonstrate your ballet dance, or videotape a tennis match in which you played, commendations, patents, licenses, or other work samples.

The following example is the actual writing of a student who received credit for her experiences and college equivalent learning. This portion of writing is an excerpt from her Portfolio, which included over 32 pages of material to earn this one 3.0 class credit.

Portfolios are not EASY, but can be tremendous time and cost-savers for adult students.

Portfolio for college credit: ART 212 Painting II 3.0 Credits in General Electives

Theory Content: "I joined the XXX Art Center in the years of 1969-1970. We had classes doing different styles of drawing - one was life drawing. I tried acrylic painting and didn't care for it, because it dries too fast. I like painting with oils.

We had a workshop given by the well-known artist Mr. XXX. He had painted all of the 14,000 ft. peaks, in Colorado. He paints beautiful realism.

We reviewed the book, Artists Handbook on Materials and Techniques, by Ralph Mayer. We drew and painted a large rock alongside of Moraine Pool. This is a scene in Rocky

Mountain National Park, on a trail from Beaver Meadows to South Bear Lake. He taught us many mixes of color (see notes from the class). He taught us to paint in the color of the rocks, and then use a black wash over the wet paint, to give the water a transparent look. When the paint was dry, we would paint a single white stroke down the center of the stream for a ripple effect."

Experience Based: "I noticed that Mr. XXX wasn't putting much detail into the rock, in the right foreground, but I began to detail mine. I put in all the cracks, lines, and lichen that you find in rocks. When Mr. XXX noticed what I was doing he went back to the front of the class and started detailing his rock. It seems that he was going to leave the rock rather abstract, but since it was in the foreground and I'm a detailed artist, I felt it should have more detail (see page XII).

We had a juried show and we could submit one of our paintings to be critiqued; if they felt it was good, it would be hung in the big show. I entered my painting of a fisherman, fishing in a stream (see page XII). This scene was taken from Empire Magazine - Sunday Paper in the Denver Post. My painting was chosen to be hung. I didn't win a prize, but received compliments on my painting. One compliment was from a well-known artist whose work I admired, Mr. XXX. He told me he really liked my work and my style of painting. I learned much about mixing colors and using surface washes, in this workshop.

After my workshop, I continued to paint and I attended Art Shows. Unfortunately, I did not take photographs of all of my paintings."

Documentation Provided: "The painting on page XIII, was done from a 3" X 3" black and white print. This was a challenge, because I had to figure out colors - soil in Illinois is black. I hadn't painted people and here I was painting my dad. It does look like him, so I was pleased.

I was commissioned to do the paintings on page XIV-XV. The lady ordered three scenes, but the third photograph did not turn out. These paintings were done in a smaller size, which I enjoyed doing. I was also commissioned to do the painting shown on page XVIII. This scene was taken from a Coors Beer advertisement. The lady liked the green water in the picture.

The next three paintings were again done from Colorado scenes, and done in fall colors. The painting on page XX, was my best trade. I received an expensive antique baby doll for this painting, but it served a therapeutic value as well. The lady I made the trade with had mental problems and when she was depressed she would sit and look at the painting. She said it would help to lift her spirits."

Now it's your turn.

EXERCISE: Portfolio Process
Choose a course description from the list you just developed and write about your knowledge in both a "theory" based and "experience" based learning. Follow the previous example, using the worksheets provided on the next few pages.

This exercise will strengthen your writing skills, and help you focus on your accomplishments.

I. My Portfolio For College Credit:

Course Title:_____ Course Number/Dept.:_____

Theory:_____

_____

_____

_____

_____

_____

_____

_____

_____

_____

_____

_____

_____

_____

_____

_____

_____

_____

_____

_____

_____

_____

_____

_____

_____

_____

_____

_____

_____

Experiences:_____

_____

_____

_____

_____

_____

_____

_____

_____

_____

_____

_____

_____

_____

_____

_____

_____

_____

_____

_____

Documentation(s):_____

_____

_____

_____

_____

_____

_____

_____

_____

_____

_____

_____

_____

_____

_____

_____

_____

Don't forget that you can use creative ways to document your learning – pictures, awards, video tape, audio tape, performance, sculptors, writings (poetry, novel), photography, technical report, project completion, wood work, construction, design models, graphic charts, samples of a product or cooking, and many more.

II. My Portfolio for College Credit:

Course Title: _____ Course #/Department: _____

Theory: _____
_____
_____
_____
_____
_____
_____
_____
_____
_____
_____
_____
_____
_____
_____
_____
_____
_____

Experiences: _____
_____
_____
_____
_____
_____
_____
_____
_____
_____
_____
_____
_____

Documentation(s): _____
_____
_____
_____
_____

_____

Now, you have an idea of the type of requirements necessary to achieve college credit for your prior learning. You may "own" college credit and not even realize it. By researching some of these nontraditional methods of gaining college credit mentioned in this chapter - ACE credits, PONSI credits, Testing Programs, and the Portfolio process - you may be much closer to achieving your degree.

By the way, the national average of awarded credit for all "Prior Learning Assessment" options has rise to 21.0 college credits – this is almost a full year of college work. So, don't say you don't have any "college knowledge", because you probably do!

Questions to ask a College Academic Advisor or Admissions Counselor:

1. Does your college adhere to the recommendations provided by the ACE and PONSI guides for military and corporate training programs? Will you evaluate my credentials for such credit?

2. Does your campus offer national exams programs such as the CLEP and PEP exams? Placement exams? Challenge exams? How can I make use of these opportunities?

3. Does your college offer the Portfolio process or ways to demonstrate my life experiences that are equivalent to college courses? Do you offer a class to help me develop my Portfolio for college credit?

Gaining college credit for what you already know
will save you time and money to achieve your goal.

Notes about this chapter:

CHAPTER FOUR – DISTANCE LEARNING

You have now checked all the sources for earning credit for your college equivalent learning. It's time to continue learning new things. You are familiar with classroom the format. However, learning can be obtained through many "nontraditional" environments and methods. You will be especially interested in these nontraditional learning options if you:

- Travel frequently
- Have young children
- Live in a remote area
- Have a physical disability
- Work irregular hours
- Prefer learning independently
- Can't find the right degree program locally

This chapter will explore alternative ways to learn that you may not have known existed.

- Telecourses on PBS, cable, satellite broadcast, or video
- Correspondence courses
- Computer Assisted Instruction
- External degree programs and "Banking" college credit
- Online courses

Telecourses

Do you like to follow an interesting series on public or educational TV? Do you subscribe to a Cable network? If you answer "yes" to these questions, you may be interested in taking a Telecourse. Colleges and Universities throughout the U.S. have developed very interesting, entertaining, and high-quality courses that are aired through Public Broadcasting Station (PBS) and local Cable stations. They are very well produced and contract moderators such as Carl Sagen, Mia Angelou, prominent historians and professors. They are quite entertaining. You probably have watched a college telecourse and didn't even know you could get college credit for this TV show. However, for college credit, you will need to do more than watch TV.

A Telecourse may be one of the most convenient and entertaining ways to earn college credit. A Telecourse consists of a series of aired broadcasts, usually 30-90 minutes in length, and they follow a planned course of instruction. Some popular Telecourse topics are: General Psychology, Economics, Art History, Ethics in America, Writing for English, etc. You may enroll at a nearby college that participates in the Telecourse programs in your area. Tuition costs vary. You will receive a textbook, course outline, assignments, and test schedules just like a "classroom" class. Many times you can receive all this information in the mail or stop by the campus and pick up your materials.

Requirements for the course vary with the instructor; some handle all the tests and assignments via the mail and telephone, while others require a few campus meetings for seminars or for examinations. The sponsoring campus may have videocassettes of the Telecourse that you can take home, or you can tape the Telecourse with your VCR for repeat viewing. These Telecourses usually last a full term.

Cautions:

- Telecourses are rigorous; they are not a "give me" credit.
- Study time should average about 3 hours for each hour of viewing time.
- Course work must be completed on a weekly basis and can be quite demanding.
- You must be self-motivated to learn on your own and preferably have a matching learning style.
- Not all colleges accept telecourse credit. Check with your advisor first, if you plan to transfer telecourse credit from another institution.

Some colleges offer complete degree programs through cable networks or live satellite classes available in homes and offices. Other campuses offer degree programs through videotaping of the actual classroom course for learning at your own pace. Examples of some of these Adult Learner Degree Programs are outlined in the Resource Guide at the back of the book.

EXERCISE: Telecourses

Call your local PBS station or local colleges for a schedule of telecourses offered. Select a course that fits into your degree program and watch a couple of shows. Do you think you would like to take courses by television? Would you prefer to take a few courses or earn your entire degree this way?

Correspondence Courses

Would you like to learn and earn college credit on your own time and at your own pace wherever you live or travel? You might find that Independent Study through correspondence courses will fit your needs. You can take a course at a distance, enrolling by mail and using the textbook, course outline, and reference materials to complete assignments and examinations – all by mail.

Correspondence courses help to:

- Upgrade your skills and knowledge
- Meet graduation requirements
- Obtain or renew a teaching certificate
- Meet licensing requirements
- Develop personal interests

You can set your own pace, since independent study often allows you to begin courses at any time and to complete them within one year. Most local colleges and state universities offer college credit by correspondence.

Once again, you will need self-motivation and self-discipline to complete course work by correspondence, but the convenience of doing it yourself on your own schedule may meet your needs. If you want to transfer correspondence courses to another campus, ask the receiving institution if they accept credits for correspondence courses—before you take the course.

EXERCISE: Correspondence Courses

Check your college Catalog and Schedule of Courses for information on correspondence courses. You find also find their policy for *transferring* correspondence credit.

Most states have at least one major public university that offers correspondence courses. You may find these courses listed under the Contact the Continuing Education department and can request a separate catalog of courses available through correspondence.
After you read the college information, answer the following questions:

1. Are there courses that fit into your degree program that you would like to take by correspondence?

2. Are you interested in pursuing an entire degree by correspondence?

Online Courses

Prior to 1996 the availability of online courses was extremely limited. With the explosion of interest in the Internet and the World Wide Web, there are now tens-of-thousands of online college courses, and hundreds of full degree programs though the internet.

Each course comes with a textbook, course outline, and a series of learning activities to be completed online or sent to the assigned instructor through electronic mail for grading. You may be required to attend online "lectures" and discussion groups with students from all over the country or around the world.

Some online courses are time specific, requiring you to complete the course work within the regular term. Others are entirely self-paced. You may find that completing an entire degree program is very isolating. If so, you may want to take some individual courses to complete degree requirements with your college, or use as transfer credit. Many online degree programs allow you to "mix and match" internet courses with actual classroom attendance.

Hardware and software requirements for online instruction will vary. Some online courses are designed to integrate with large corporate computer systems, such as UNIX or other platforms. Most can be accessed through your personal internet Service Provider (ISP) such as AOL, YAHOO, HotMail, Earthlink, and many others.

You must keep up with your studies, but you have the support of others "online" in a classroom. Often these courses have discussion groups (online) and "chat" rooms. OnLine classes may be a good way for you to earn credit at your worksite or in your home.

The best way to find information about online courses is - *online!*

Here are some websites with listings of online courses and full college degrees –

Remember, these databases ONLY have those colleges represented that pay to be in their databases....not all potential colleges/universities will be listed!

www.ecollege.com

www.petersons.com

NOTES:

EXERCISE: OnLine Courses

Log onto your ISP and visit the online college search sites listed above.

Search for the courses or degree programs that interest you. Click on the college(s) that interest you and open up additional information about your selections. You should also continue your investigation by searching each college's website.

After you read the information about available online options, answer the following questions:

1. Will these courses transfer to my college/university?
2. Will these courses fulfill any of my degree requirements?
3. Are you interested in pursuing an entire degree online?

New online classes and degree programs appear almost daily. If you can't find what you want, don't give up. Keep checking for updated information.

"Banking" College Credit

Have you moved from city to city for your job or the military? Maybe you have taken courses at many different colleges, because you have not been able to stay in one town long enough to complete your degree. Each time you move do you seem to start over trying to fulfill the residency and degree requirements at yet another campus? Or, maybe you have changed your major over a dozen times during the course of your studies. For whatever reason you may have lots of college credits, but no degree.

Several institutions of higher education will "bank" your credits from any regionally accredited institution, allowing you to fulfill all their degree requirements without ever setting foot on their campus or taking a single course from them.

Excelsior College (formerly Regents College) in New York state, and Thomas Edison State College in New Jersey are two of the most widely recognized credit banking institutions. Each offers degrees in many different majors. These schools have no traditional classes or campus, and there are no residency requirements.

These colleges establish their own degree requirements, but will accept transfer credits to fulfill each and every course they require to grant a college degree. You could have taken courses at dozens of other colleges/universities, but these institutions will be the one to actually issue your college degree. If you own a lot of college credit, you may want to investigate their requirements for a General Studies, or Liberal Arts degree. Often times these programs are most flexible for the choice of courses to complete their requirements. We have advised students who already "owned" an Associate or Bachelor's degree, but didn't know it. The student merely had to send official transcripts of all their college credits, pay some fees, complete a "graduation application" and within weeks their college degree was issued and sent by one of these colleges. They were thrilled!

EXERCISE: Learning Profile

Use your word-processing software, or sheets of paper, and list all your college courses – you want to also put the number of the course, grade, and institution. Then, keep the list going by writing in all your training courses – then, any certificates or licenses (real estate license, life-savings certification, private pilot license, C++ software certification, etc.). Add to the list your skills as defined by your resume – communication and writing skills, management skills, negotiating skills, leadership qualities, etc. Finally list areas in which you have expertise – tennis, piano, own a small business, art, music, volunteer work, etc.

Once you see all you skills, talents, and learning put on one long list, you might just impress yourself! This list will help you "visually" see all your accomplishments and help determine the options in higher education you need and want from a potential college. This "summary" is also a good, condensed source of information about you, to present to potential employers.

External Degree Programs

A college degree can be obtained by working adults, and other part-time students, through external degree programs. These programs may be located at "extended campus" sites, throughout your city, state or country. External degree programs may refer to any programs that are not located on their "home" campus. Such classes may be offered through self-directed planned study, telecourses, independent study, correspondence, computer, workshops, or classes on military bases, at your work site, internships, or by practicums. Credit may be earned from prior learning, by transfer of course credits, and by documented learning from experience (work, community service, self-directed learning projects, travel).
State boundaries no longer limit college and university curriculum. State education may have an entire "system" of colleges in place to "share" courses that are in common for any degree requirements. They may also have coordinating locations throughout the state or via OnLine courses.

More Ways To Learn

We recommend that you contact a number of schools, get their catalogs, and compare their offerings. You can combine ways to earn credits on your timetable and on your own budget. More often than not, adult learners spend more time on research and comparison-shopping for their family automobile than they do for their continued education which affects their careers throughout their entire life!

Depending on your schedule, you may want to actually attend classes during the day with the younger college students. Courses offered during the day require two or three days of attendance each week, for one or two hours for each classroom "period".

Programs for adult learners may be offered on a **weekend** format consisting of class periods on a Friday evening, a Saturday or Sunday morning. Each class period may last three to five hours. Weekend classes may be offered every weekend or every other weekend, with much independent work (reading and writing) expected from the student during the days/weeks in between classroom meeting times. Other colleges offer courses on an **accelerated** or **self-paced** situation. Classroom times might be one evening per week in blocks of three or four hours. The same curriculum must be covered within this condensed timeframe, so you will be doing lots of independent study. Self-paced work may include attending a "lab" setting at the college where computer use and study "carrels" are used by each student. These types of options are not any easier than the traditional daytime classes. They just may be more suited to your lifestyle. If you do not have a job at present, then **cooperative education, work/study**, **internships**, **practicums** or **independent study** may be useful for you. These options allow students to earn college credit for experiential learning—combining "theory" or textbook learning with the practical element of trying out your learning in an organization or work situation. Campuses can arrange for you to work in an environment that supports your learning in a particular area of study. An example might be an adult student taking a college course in Abnormal Psychology and earning credit for working (volunteer or paid work) in a mental health center, or taking a course on Computers and working in a corporate setting. These opportunities might also get you in the door for a future full-time "paid" job upon graduation or during your part-time college study.

Some campuses offer special **Summer classes** or **Interim classes** which are offered during the traditional "break" times of the Semester or Quarter yearly calendar. The traditional student usually takes the summers off, while attending classes and living in the dorms nine out of the twelve-month school year. During the summer, many campuses conduct classes for adult students to keep their campus operating during these "off" times. The same opportunities may apply to the weeks "off" the traditional students take between each term—Winter break and Spring break. Don't go to Florida – take a course!

Questions To Ask a college Academic Advisor or Admissions Counselor:

1. Does your campus participate in any telecourse programs or do you accept credits earned through telecourse learning to transfer to your campus to fulfill degree requirements?

2. What type of programs does your campus offer in the summer? Inter-term courses? Internships? Cooperative work/study opportunities?

3. Does your campus offer correspondence courses or computer assisted learning opportunities? Will your campus transfer any of these types of methods of learning from other campuses to fulfill degree requirements?

4. What external degree programs meet my learning needs and my lifestyle?

Notes About This Chapter:

CHAPTER FIVE - PUTTING YOUR PLAN TOGETHER

Let's Review.

You have now learned what you need to know to be an informed adult consumer of higher education. It's time to start putting your knowledge to work for you. Start by completing the following exercise, keeping in mind the information you have covered so far in this guidebook.

 EXERCISE:

Complete this short "Needs and Skills Assessment"©.

1. Why do you want to go to college? (Motivation, Incentives, Career goals, Learning Needs)

2. Do you want to pursue training, degree or personal knowledge gain?

3. Which degree are you seeking (Associate, undergraduate or graduate)? Which major area of study? What is the highest level of degree you ever hope to attain?

4. Describe the type of college you desire (small, mid-sized, large university; religious affiliation; public or private; co-educational or gender specific)?

5. Amount of money willing/able to spend on education? Does your employer offer tuition reimbursement? Are you eligible for any other educational assistance?

6. How much time do you have available to attend classes and/or study each week? When will you be able to study - that is, do you have time during the day, evenings, Weekends, lunch hour or during work hours? Is your study time available on a regular or irregular schedule? Does your available time change during different times of the year?

   List any activities that you intend to continue while pursuing your degree. These may include work, church, clubs, organizations, recreational activities, exercise, hobbies, family, etc.

7. When would you prefer to attend classes (day, evening, weekend, independent study)?

   Will this schedule need to change during different times of the year? For example, some people like weekend classes during the traditional school year, but want to keep their weekends free in the summer. In your area it might be very difficult to drive to classes during the long, dark, cold winters – so you may want to use distance learning in winter.

8. In what city will your degree be completed? Are you planning on moving during your participation in a degree program? If yes, you need to select a "portable" degree or make sure the classes you take <u>now</u> will transfer to a college in your new location.

9. Are you interested in individual learning methods (home study, self-paced courses, telecourses, independent study, online)? Which individual learning methods do you prefer? To what extent do you want to make use of these options (entire program or disbursed with more traditional classroom study)?

10. Have you had any military training for possible credit through the ACE guides?

11. Have you had any corporate training courses for possible credit in the ACE guides?

12. Would you like to make use of testing? Which exams, and for what classes? (CLEP, TECEP, Ohio University, Challenge, others)

13. Would you like to make use of your life learning experiences through the "Portfolio" process? Which subjects do you think you know well enough to obtain possible college credit?

14. Have you attended any institutions of higher education? What classes appear to be transferable to another institution?

Notes on this Section:

Now that you have decided on your major, selected learning resources, and narrowed down your list of schools - it is time to design your degree program. Included in this section are several copies of a Requirement Checklist. You should complete one for each college you are considering and then compare your findings. On the following pages we will go through a "sample" Requirement Checklist (section by section), to help you become familiar with the process.

Before going any further, assemble the materials you will need to complete the exercises that follow. You will need the college catalog for each school you are considering, the requirements for the programs you are considering, transcripts from all institutions you have attended, and information for non-traditional credit options, such as:

- CLEP
- Correspondence courses
- Telecourses
- Online courses
- Portfolio credit, etc.

All colleges will have certain requirements which every student must meet to complete most any degree program. Typically, these include:

- General education requirements
- Major courses
- Upper and lower division credits
- General electives
- Minor or concentration of courses

General Education

A bachelor's degree should provide you with a well-rounded education. This includes coursework from a broad range of topics. General education requirements may include coursework in English, Math, Science, Humanities and Social Sciences. Remember the Liberal Arts Skills Chart way back in Chapter One? The skills we refer to there are developed in many of your General Education courses.

Check the college catalog for information on the number and type of general education credits required at each college. These requirements are very similar among colleges/universities – but, they will vary. Not only do program requirements vary, but so does the terminology they use to describe these courses. One school's "General Education" may be named the "Core" requirements at another institution.

Think about how you want to fulfill the General Education requirements. These courses are, by definition, general in content and are widely available in non-traditional options: telecourses, CLEP tests, correspondence courses, etc. You might want to take General Education courses at your local community college or earn some credits through your portfolio.

If you have earned credits from a previous college, find out from an advisor whether they would apply toward these requirements.

Check with the college where you intend to complete your degree, and ask about their policy for accepting transfer credits. Remember that each college will define what are humanities or social science credits. History of the Egyptians may count as a social science at one school and Humanities at another.

EXERCISE: General Education

Potential College/University_____

In this section, list all general education requirements. Write down courses already completed, options for completing remaining coursework, and the number of credits still needed.

Total Number of General Education credits required _____

Required Credits	Area of study	Courses completed	Options for completion	Remaining Credits
6 credits	Composition	English 101	CLEP	3.0 credits
	Social Science			
	Science			
	Math			
	Humanities			
	Other			

Major

In this section, list all of the upper division courses required for your major, as well as lower-division prerequisites which may be required. Typically, these courses are the "Intro" courses – Introduction to Psychology, Introduction to Computers. These lower level credits may also fulfill one or more General Education requirements. Where possible, always try to "double-dip" in this fashion - use a course to fulfill several requirements at the same time. Indicate if you have already completed any of these courses and where you intend to take them. The major courses are probably the most difficult to transfer, so you will want to take most of these courses at the college where you expect to earn your degree.

Name of Major (Example: History, Management) _____

Total number of Major credits required (Example: 24.0) _____

Required Credits	Area of Study	Courses/Credits Completed	Options for Completion	Remaining Credits
6 credits	*lower level prerequisites*	*History 101*	*Telecourse*	*3.0 credits*
3 credits	*History 300*	*History 300*	*---*	*0 credits*

Minor

Repeat the same process for a Minor or Concentration of courses (if required). Usually, this grouping of subjects is no more than 4-5 courses. A Minor allows an in-depth study of a particular area of interest.

Name of Minor (Example: Communications) _____

Total number of Minor credits required (Example: 12) _____

Required Credits	Area of Study	Courses/Credits Completed	Options for Completion	Remaining Credits
3 credits	Comm. 301	---	Comm. 301	3.0 credits
3 credits				
3 credits				
3 credits				

Additional Upper-Division Electives (if required)

Most four-year schools have a minimum number of upper level (300 or above) credit required for graduation. The number will include courses in the major, minor, and perhaps additional upper-level electives. List all of the upper division electives required (if any). Could coursework from previous institutions apply? What about PONSI credits? Portfolio?

Number of Upper Division Electives required (Example: 30.0) _____

Required Credits	Area of Study	Courses Completed	Options for Completion	Remaining Credits
3 credits	History 300	History 300	---	---
3 credits	Comm. 301	Comm. 301	---	---
3 credits	Pol. Sci. 312	---	Portfolio	3.0 credits

General Electives

General Electives are courses that the student has the most choice for selection. Here you can choose courses in area such as Archery, Poetry of the Middle Ages or more career-oriented classes.

General Electives (usually) can be in any subject area. If your degree will be in business administration and your company does business with a number of Japanese companies, it would make sense to take coursework in Japanese language and culture and in international business law. Maybe you want a degree in computer science so that you can start a business teaching other small business owners how to use computers and software. You might consider taking courses in starting a small business and in teaching methods for adult students. Many people who major in fine arts areas, such as photography, dance or textiles might also want to take business and marketing courses to help them start a studio.

List all of the general electives (100-400 level) required (if any) for your degree and indicate if any of these requirements can be met through transfer courses from previous colleges. Again, think about how you want to earn these credits. Is portfolio a possibility? What about CLEP test? PONSI credits? Telecourses?

Notes:

Number of General Electives Required (Example: 30.0) _____

Required Credits	Area of Study	Courses Completed	Options for Completion	Remaining Credits

Requirement Checklist

Every institution of higher education will have a Requirement Checklist listing all the required courses needed for graduation. Yes, even elective credits are "required" in this sense. Academic advisors use these "ReqChecks" to determine each student's status for degree completion. This checklist outlines all the course requirements for each degree program. Advisors "fill-in" those charts with courses as they are successfully completed by the student. Credit for courses from transfer credit are also listed. Eventually, the student will have all their requirements fulfilled and can apply for graduation!

You can use the following "generic" requirement checklists to determine your status with each institution that you are considering receiving your degree. The final determination for transfer credit rests with the "official" evaluation done by each institution. However, you can use these forms to develop an educational plan which represents an estimate of your credits, and time/money needed to complete an institution's graduation requirements.

The following is an example of how you can use the information you have learned in this guidebook to create your PERSONAL EDUCATIONAL PLAN. You do not have to rely on the college recruiter to develop your plan. College recruiters/advisors will not be able to "network" options for learning - they are only allowed to recommend their institution's courses to complete your <u>entire</u> degree. College administrators frown on their employees suggesting competitors, if it they know you would be better off at another institution. Business is business. Remember, that you should have your plan reviewed and approved by the <u>college from which you plan to earn your degree</u>. They can check your work and make sure that your plan will be effective in completing your degree.

Notes on this Section:

EXERCISE: Designing your Personal Education Plan

1. **INSTITUTION:** (College from which you plan to receive your degree; the college which meets most of your learning needs)

   Whatsa Matter U.--WMUniversity

2. **GENERAL EDUCATION** (30.0)

Required Credits	Area of Study	Courses Completed	Courses Needed and Options for Completion
6.0	Communication	ENG 101 (3/T)	ENG 102 (3)--CLEP
6.0	Social Science	0	PSY 100 (3)--TV ,HIS 210 (3) TV
6.0	Math/Science	0	MTH 200 (3)-GEOL 100 (3)-Online
6.0	Humanities	ART 101 (3/T)	HUM 100 (3)--CLEP
6.0	Elective	0	SOC 100 (3)--TV
			PSY 200 (3)--TV

(Note: This student had taken an English Composition course from another institution several years earlier--ENG 101 (3.0 credits)--which will transfer (T) into WMU. This student plans to take a CLEP test to complete the remaining credits, as her communication and writing skills are excellent. She has chosen to complete her Social Science courses by taking classes offered by a local community college via the television and then transfer those credits to WMU. She has no credit in the Math/Science category and plans to take those courses from another local university that offers correspondence courses, and again, transfer those credits to WMU. This student had taken ART 101 several years ago from another institution and will transfer those credits to WMU, while planning to take a CLEP test in the humanities to fulfill another 3.0 credits in this category. This college allows students to take 6.0 credits of their choice as electives in the general studies area. She will take Sociology 100 and Psychology 200 by telecourses from the local community college and transfer them to WMU. Notice that this student will not take any of these requirements from the college where she plans to graduate.)

3. **MAJOR**-- Business Administration (15.0)

Required Credits	Area of Study	Courses Completed	Courses Needed and Options for Completion
3.0	Bus. Ethics 300	3	WMU (3)
3.0	Marketing 310	0	WMU (3)
3.0	Statistics 360	0	WMU (3)
3.0	Bus Law 340	0	WMU (3)
3.0	Adv. Managt.400	0	WMU (3)--Portfolio

(Note: This student is planning to take all of her major courses of study with WMU. She has completed Introduction to Business with WMU. She will try to receive credit for Introduction to Management through the portfolio process offered at WMU.)

4. **MINOR** (required) --Management (12.0)

Required Credits	Area of Study	Courses Completed	Courses Needed and Options for Completion
3.0	Intro. Mgt. 210	0	WMU--Portfolio
3.0	Supr. Skills 101	0	WMU--Portfolio
3.0	Personnel 101	0	WMU
3.0	Mang. Tech.210	0	WMU--Portfolio

(Note: This student is planning to take all of her minor courses of study with WMU. She will attempt to gain credits for three of these courses through the portfolio process.)

5. **UPPER DIVISION ELECTIVES**--Courses in the 300-400 level chosen by the student in the Business field of study. (15.0)

Required Credits	Area of Study	Courses Completed	Courses Needed and Options for Completion
3.0	Prin. Mktg. 300	3	Transferred
3.0	Bus. Law 310	3	Transferred
3.0	Statistics 312	0	WMU
3.0	Intl. Bus. 355	0	WMU

(Note: This student has taken two courses at another institution in the past and transferred these courses to WMU. She will take two WMU courses in the evenings)

6. **GENERAL ELECTIVES**--These are courses in which the student has almost free reign in determining what areas of study they would like to choose. These courses may relate to their major field of study or be totally unrelated to broaden their education. (45.0 credits)

Required Credits	Area of Study	Courses Completed	Courses Needed and Options for Completion
3	Training	3	ACE/Corporate
3	Communications	3	ACE/Corporate
3	Physical Ed.	3	ACE/Military
6	Human Resources	6	TECE exams
6	Spanish	6	CLEP exams
9	Music	9	WMU--Portfolio
6	Computers	6	WMU--Portfolio
3	History	3	TV
3	Literature	0	TV (3)
3	Finance in Bus.	0	WMU (3)

(Note: This student will use a variety of educational options to fulfill her general electives. She will take one course in Finance at WMU on the weekends. She will complete two courses through the Portfolio process at WMU. Her remaining credits will come from courses she has completed that are recommended for credit by the ACE guides, PEP exams and CLEP exams.)

This student now has a "recipe" to follow to complete her degree using many more options than WMU offers. She has a course-by-course plan to earn her degree. If she follows this plan, she will meet the requirements of WMU for graduation. She has used time-savings options:

- TV courses at home,
- Correspondence courses at home,
- Testing options
- ACE credits,
- Portfolio credits

and cost-saving options:

- TV courses through the community college,
- Testing options
- ACE credits,
- Portfolio credits.

Being aware of all your options for education, lets you create a personalized educational plan that is time and cost effective!

The next few pages offer you the opportunity to develop your own personal educational plan. Use the previous example to network local and national opportunities available to you to create a plan that is best for you.

NETWORK YOUR OPTIONS FOR COST & TIME SAVINGS !

Degree Plan - Example:
Requirement Checklist

College or University: XYZ College

General Studies:

6	Communications	CLEP
3	Social Science	Online Courses
3	Humanities	TeleCourses
6	Math/Science	CLEP

Major: Business Administration

6	Accounting I&II	Classroom Course
6	Computer Science	TECEP Exan
3	Business Law	OnLine Course
6	Mico/Macro Economics	Classroom Courses
3	Management	Portfolio
3	Marketing	Challenge Exam
3	Finance	Classroom Course

Minor: Management

3	Leadership	Accelerated Course
3	Labor Issues	Portfolio
3	International Business	Accelerated Course
3	Project Management	Ohio U. Test

General Electives: Business & Other

12	Military Science	ACE credits
9	Technical/Applied Credits	Transfer courses
6	Music	Portfolio
6	Foreign Language	CLEP

REQUIREMENT CHECKLIST:

Institution: _____

General Studies: Required fields of study

Credits	Area of Study	Courses Completed	Credits Needed	Method to Complete
___	_____	___ ___ ___	_____	_____
___	_____	___ ___ ___	_____	_____
___	_____	___ ___ ___	_____	_____
___	_____	___ ___ ___	_____	_____
___	_____	___ ___ ___	_____	_____
___	_____	___ ___ ___	_____	_____

Major: _____

___	_____	___ ___ ___	_____	_____
___	_____	___ ___ ___	_____	_____
___	_____	___ ___ ___	_____	_____
___	_____	___ ___ ___	_____	_____
___	_____	___ ___ ___	_____	_____
___	_____	___ ___ ___	_____	_____
___	_____	___ ___ ___	_____	_____
___	_____	___ ___ ___	_____	_____
___	_____	___ ___ ___	_____	_____
___	_____	___ ___ ___	_____	_____

Concentration/Minor/Additional Required Lower-Division Courses:

___	_____	___ ___ ___	_____	_____
___	_____	___ ___ ___	_____	_____
___	_____	___ ___ ___	_____	_____
___	_____	___ ___ ___	_____	_____

General Electives: Required Courses and/or free choice:

___	_____	___ ___ ___	_____	_____
___	_____	___ ___ ___	_____	_____
___	_____	___ ___ ___	_____	_____
___	_____	___ ___ ___	_____	_____
___	_____	___ ___ ___	_____	_____
___	_____	___ ___ ___	_____	_____
___	_____	___ ___ ___	_____	_____
___	_____	___ ___ ___	_____	_____

REQUIREMENT CHECKLIST:

Institution: _____

General Studies: Required fields of study

Credits	Area of Study	Courses Completed	Credits Needed	Method to Complete
_____	_____	____ ____ ____	_____	_____
_____	_____	____ ____ ____	_____	_____
_____	_____	____ ____ ____	_____	_____
_____	_____	____ ____ ____	_____	_____
_____	_____	____ ____ ____	_____	_____
_____	_____	____ ____ ____	_____	_____

Major: _____

_____	_____	____ ____ ____	_____	_____
_____	_____	____ ____ ____	_____	_____
_____	_____	____ ____ ____	_____	_____
_____	_____	____ ____ ____	_____	_____
_____	_____	____ ____ ____	_____	_____
_____	_____	____ ____ ____	_____	_____
_____	_____	____ ____ ____	_____	_____
_____	_____	____ ____ ____	_____	_____
_____	_____	____ ____ ____	_____	_____

Concentration/Minor/Additional Required Lower-Division Courses:

_____	_____	____ ____ ____	_____	_____
_____	_____	____ ____ ____	_____	_____
_____	_____	____ ____ ____	_____	_____
_____	_____	____ ____ ____	_____	_____

General Electives: Required Courses and/or free choice:

_____	_____	____ ____ ____	_____	_____
_____	_____	____ ____ ____	_____	_____
_____	_____	____ ____ ____	_____	_____
_____	_____	____ ____ ____	_____	_____
_____	_____	____ ____ ____	_____	_____
_____	_____	____ ____ ____	_____	_____
_____	_____	____ ____ ____	_____	_____
_____	_____	____ ____ ____	_____	_____

CONGRATULATIONS--YOU CAN DO IT!

You have just completed a most important part of "going back to school" - that is the time and effort needed to do proper planning. Without this effort you could spend a lot more time and money than may be necessary to complete your education, and earn the degree that you have wanted for a long time.

Now that you have completed your educational plans, you probably have a much better idea of which college is best suited for your needs. You also are aware of the many options in your community or across the nation that you can USE to complete you degree plan. You do not have to limit yourself to one institution. Our country has a great diversity in educational opportunities--make use of that opportunity. By being a better "consumer" of higher education you can tailor-make an educational plan to match your career goals, learning style, prior learning, and time and cost budgets.

You have taken a big step to make your education a successful experience. Your work is not over. You have decided to take on a major commitment in your life--completing your college degree. You will find many challenges as you proceed, but also many rewards and accomplishments. A college education provides the credentials for success so necessary in today's economy. Your education will also give you a broader vision of the world and its complexity, and will bring you a deeper understanding of yourself.

We hope you have learned about many new resources and opportunities waiting for you in higher education. We also hope you have learned one most important lesson - - -

YOU ARE NEVER

TOO OLD
TOO BUSY
TOO BROKE
TOO SCARED

TO COMPLETE YOUR COLLEGE DEGREE

CHAPTER SIX - GRADUATE SCHOOL

What's Next?

Lifelong Learning Is Not A Trend – It's A Necessity

Many adults who earned their bachelor's degree a while back in time thought - maybe even vowed! - they would never set foot in college again. Oh, contraire! Adult learners are racing to enter Graduate and Professional Schools too. Many find that their career direction is finally clear, or that it has changed, or maybe they need new skills to move up. Or, perhaps it is now YOUR time to learn for fun, and personal enrichment. For contemplate graduate school, before the ink is even dry on their undergraduate diploma. Studies show that the more education you acquire, the more you will want. Where do you fit?

We hope that if you used this book to chart your undergraduate education, you were careful to look ahead to the possibility of graduate school. If so, you have taken the necessary prerequisite courses for admission to your program of choice.

If you hope to move on to a different job, contact 2-3 people who are in a position to hire you for that future job. Show them the curriculum for the nontraditional degree you are considering and ask them if that degree would qualify you for the position you desire. It is important to obtain more than one opinion because people have their own individual prejudice.

If you are returning to higher education for Graduate School, after a long absence, we welcome you to the back! You will find that the options available to you are far greater than when you left campus a few, or many years ago.

It is yet another process to select the best-fit Graduate or Professional School. Many of the same understandings about "yourself" (Chapters 1-4) are needed for proper Graduate School decisions.

What follows are some conditions and issues that are unique to the graduate/professional school application process.

Some colleges will accept you into a Graduate program
if you've completed 90.0 semester credits of undergraduate coursework
<u>and</u> have extensive, relevant work experience
without actually completing an undergraduate degree

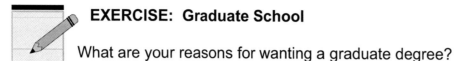

EXERCISE: Graduate School

What are your reasons for wanting a graduate degree?

Take your time to answer this question – it may serve as an outline for your "Purpose Statement" for many Graduate applications.

Admission Requirements

Most graduate and professional programs require an admission exam and review of your undergraduate record as part of the application process. Many programs may also require letters of reference and admission essays. Some schools realize that these tests do not necessarily measure what needs to be measured of the adult student. They no longer require any admission tests for adult learners.

The admission exams for Graduate School are usually the GMAT (Graduate Management Aptitude Test) for school of Business, or the GRE (Graduate Record Exam) for other areas of study. Again, be a consumer. If the thought of an admission test is too daunting, look for a program that does not require one. However, if the program you *really* want requires one, don't avoid it for only this reason.

Proponents of admission exams argue that because they are "standardized" they are more objective than grades or letters of recommendation. In other words, everyone applicant is measured by the same criteria. Opponents note that tests may inadvertently be biased with regard to gender, race, or ethnicity, and are therefore anything but "standardized". For most adults who completed their Bachelor degree years ago, these tests are not a good measure to determine their abilities to succeed in Graduate School. Colleges/Universities that are committed to the adult learner usually recognize this, and select other criteria to review for admission purposes

Below are brief descriptions of the standard admission exams used by Graduate and Professional Schools. All of them are given only a few times a year at selected test centers. Registration for these exams will occur weeks or months in advance.

EXERCISE: Graduate School Profile

Complete the following information for each graduate school you are considering attending. Define your major area of study for each program. Record admissions tests which are required and determine if these exams are absolutely necessary for an adult student. Are there certain prerequisite courses required for admission? These are courses that you must have completed in your undergraduate degree, or still need to take to qualify for the Graduate program. Investigate any additional admissions requirements (letters of recommendation, statement of purpose, etc.) needed.

College/University: _____

Degree/Major (i.e., MBA or Finance): _____

Admission Test(s) Required: _____

Letters of Recommendation Required (How many? Format? From past Professors? Employment? etc.) _____

_____

Prerequisite Coursework (List courses): _____
_____
_____

Statement of Purpose: Your reasons to enroll in Graduate School (length will vary):
_____
_____
_____
_____
_____
_____
_____
_____
_____
_____
_____
_____
_____
_____
_____
_____
_____
_____

GMAT- Graduate Management Admission Test

GMAT (Graduate Management Admission Test) scores are used as part of the evaluation process by many colleges/universities for admission to their School of Business. The GMAT exam accesses certain skills, more so than the applicant's knowledge of business or management principles. The Verbal Skills portion of the exam measures reading comprehension, sentence correction, and critical reasoning. The Quantitative Skills portion includes problem solving abilities and data/math sufficiency.

When you take the GMAT, you need to designate the school(s) that you want GMAT to send your scores. Most colleges will want to receive your last two GMAT scores earned within the past five years. Thus, it is important to do your best the first time. Since most schools will average scores, it takes a great deal of improvement to dramatically alter your score.

GRE - Graduate Record Examinations

GRE (Graduate Record Examination) scores are used as part of the evaluation process by many college/universities for admission to their graduate and professional schools – other than business majors. The GRE includes both a General Test and a variety of Subject Tests. Schools requiring the GRE will specify which test(s) to take. The General Test includes sections on Verbal Ability, Quantitative Ability, and Analytical Ability. The General Test measures ability or aptitude--not knowledge of a subject area. The numerous Subject Tests are designed to cover an entire specialized field, such as Chemistry, Psychology, Education, and many others. The questions are broad in scope, allowing the test taker to demonstrate both knowledge and application of that field of study.

LSAT - Law School Admission Test

The LSAT (Law School Admission Test) is used by all American Bar Association-approved Law Schools in the United States. Like the GRE General Test and the GMAT, it does not measure knowledge in a specific area (no, you are not expected to know about torts and contracts). Rather, it tests your ability in the areas of Reading Comprehension (1 section), Analytical Reasoning (1 section), and Logical Reasoning (2 sections). Finally, there is a required 30 minute Writing Sample which is not scored by the testing service, but sent on to the law schools you designate, for their evaluation. There are many "correspondence" schools of law springing up on the internet. Be wary of their accreditation if they do not require the LSAT exam for admission.

MAT - Miller Analogies Test

The MAT (Miller Analogies Test) is becoming more popular with many graduate schools, instead of the GMAT or the GRE. The one hundred itemed, fifty minute, multiple-choice test measures higher-level intellectual problem-solving skills. The questions are in the form of analogies. The test-taker must choose the correct response from those given. In order to do so, the individual needs to know the definitions of the words, as well as the relationship between the paired words. For example, if shown "cat:fur::bird:? What would the correct correlation be from the choices of : dog, food, air, or feathers. The question would be read as, "cat is to fur as bird is to? Of course, the correct response would be "feathers". The questions cover a wide range of subject areas, with no one area receiving greater weight in questions. All of the items are of uniform difficulty.

MCAT--Medical College Admission Test

The MCAT (Medical College Admission Test) is used, in concert with many other factors, to evaluate applicants for admission to medical schools and colleges. It is a test of both abilities and knowledge. Unlike its counterparts (the GRE, GMAT, and LSAT) this test lasts the better part of a day. The MCAT includes the following areas: Verbal Reasoning, Physical Sciences, Writing Sample, and Biological Sciences. Normally, applicants taking the MCAT will have the equivalent of one year of college study in biology, general and/or inorganic chemistry, organic chemistry, physics, and one year of college mathematics. Although they may not say it, many medical schools are not receptive to the adult learner applicant. It takes many years of study, residency, and specialty interns to be able to become a doctor. Most adults can't afford all this time in school, and recognize that they will be near retirement age if/when they complete the learning.

Test Preparation Courses

Test preparation courses have become big business. If you have been anywhere near a college campus you have seen advertisements in the student newspaper and posters in student areas for Graduate School test-prep courses. There are also several corporations that have very effective entrance exam preparatory courses. Kaplan, Inc. has proven great results – even raises scores by 20,30, or more points. They are expensive, but may be worth the cost.

Should you sign up for such a course? Will it help your performance? Is it worth the money? What about the many test preparation books available? There are no easy answers. A lot depends on your *learning style,* which we talked about in Chapter One, as well as your individual commitment and self-discipline. For students who need the security of a traditional learning environment, a preparation course may be useful. Surrounded by other students and led by an instructor those who are more comfortable in a conventional learning atmosphere may benefit. If, on the other hand, you work well independently, are self-motivated, can enjoy and adapt to a flexible schedule and learning environment, you may be well-served to use one of the many preparation books or computer programs available. Many Graduate Schools offer preparation courses for their "new recruits". You can compare these courses to the commercial preparation courses to make your decision.

Resources Available Online

Wow! There is good news for students who use their computers for everything from paying bills to taking classes. We went online to discover what was available to students preparing for the various entrance tests we have just been talking about. Using the Google search engine, and searching simply for LSAT preparation (or GMAT, etc.) yielded a variety of possibilities. First of all, we discovered many listings for "test preps" online courses. We also found they have descriptions, prices, and availability of software to assist in preparing for the tests. There are also listings of courses offered on college campuses and throughout communities. Both commercial courses and university-sponsored courses are listed. So, for the computer-literate or even the quasi-literate, the Internet can again be a valuable resource. For more information, go to: www.google.com – use keywords: "preparatory courses" GMAT or GRE or LSAT, etc.

General Guidelines

No matter how you choose to prepare for these exams, the following general guidelines need attention:

1. Find out how often the particular test you need to take is given (usually four times per year) and allow adequate time to register and prepare for it. Different schools will have different admission timetables, so determine the optimum time to register for, and take the test. Don't forget to allow adequate time for your score to be reported back to you and sent to the schools of your choice, in time for admission deadlines.

2. All of the tests mentioned above have study guides. These booklets give general test-taking hints and sample questions. These free booklets will provide an excellent starting point for your preparation, and can be sent to you by the testing company (GMAT, GRE, etc.). You can also purchase study guides at your local college/university bookstore and at most retail "chain" bookstores.

3. Take advantage of the Diagnostic Tests offered by the test preparation books or companies. These tests help identify your strengths and weaknesses. The Practice Tests closely mirror the type of questions, level of questions, and the scope of the questions you will be asked on the "real" test. Become very familiar with the Practice Tests.

4. Determine whether or not you are penalized for wrong answers. This will make a difference in your test-taking strategy. Again, the booklets that accompany your registration will tell you this.

5. The idea is to become very familiar with the types of questions and the time limits you will be up against. Practice!

6. Some schools offer practice tests. If so, take one.

On the day of the test, make sure you:

1. Are well rested.

2. Know exactly where the test will be given.

3. Arrive to the test site about 20 minutes in advance.

4. Have all necessary materials (pencils, etc.)

5. Know exactly what you are and are not allowed to bring into the exam.

6. Get comfortable with the format of the exam. This will speed you up if you are not trying to determine basic directions, which you should already know with adequate preparation.

7. Briefly scan each section of the exam before you begin it. This will allow you to slightly adjust your "time" strategy.

8. Take brief (few second) rest stops if you find yourself losing concentration. Shutting your eyes and taking a deep breath may be all you need to do, to re-focus your energy.

9. Don't become flustered. You are not supposed to know all the answers.

10. Don't spend too much time on any one question.

Coming in "The Back Door"

Okay, you just can't bring yourself to take one of these nasty-sounding tests we've just been talking about, - or you took one and didn't do well enough - or your grades (either recent or past) were not stellar. What can you do? Nothing makes an admission committee stand up and take notice like *success in their courses.* Try enrolling for a few courses in your curriculum of choice as a non-degree student and make sure you do well. How can they argue with good grades in the *very courses* that are required of your chosen program! Find out the maximum number of credits you can take as a non-degree student. You want to make sure all of your coursework will apply to your degree program, once you are admitted.

Raising Your GPA

As we mentioned earlier, you can always repeat courses you did poorly in, to get higher grades recorded on your transcript. Just make sure you do well the second time around! Some schools will average all your grades, while others will take just the most recent grades. Either way, you are proving your ability and desire. There will be schools that require a certain (minimal) GPA for admission. If they have no restriction on the level, or subject matter of your courses - take courses you enjoy and know that you will do well so you are more assured of receiving a good grade and raise your GPA.

Make sure you know the rules of the game before you try these strategies. Remember to be a consumer. Know exactly what you need to do for admission. Know the number of credits, the types of courses, and the grades required to boost your GPA.

Nontraditional Degree Programs

Most of what you've read in the previous chapters for undergraduate education planning, applies to graduate degrees as well. However, there are some differences. Most graduate programs only require 30.0 – 36.0 credits. Since these programs are shorter than an undergraduate degree – about 10 to 12 courses – graduate schools want you to take their curriculum. They usually do not transfer more than 1-2 courses from another graduate program. So, it is very important that you pick the right program for your needs. If you transfer to another graduate program after completing a course or two, you will lose the rest of your credits, and basically have to start over at the new school.

Graduate schools rarely grant credit for what you already know. Very few will grant credit through ACE credits or a Portfolio. Requirements are much more prescriptive at this level. There are some testing options that grant advanced level credits, but check with your

Advisor about any transfer opportunities.

Programs for the adult learner are very common throughout higher education. You will still be able to choose from a variety of *scheduling* options, including:

- Evening
- Weekend
- Accelerated
- Self-Paced

You may also select from a variety of *delivery methods:*

- Telecourses
- Correspondence courses
- Online courses
- External degrees
- Independent study
- And of course, classroom-based learning

As you become more specialized in a field of study, it is more important that you are certain your degree will enhance your career. It is important to determine whether or not a nontraditional degree will be acceptable to your current or future employer. For example, if your ultimate goal is to teach at a traditional university, you should probably earn your graduate degree(s) at a traditional institution. Why? Traditional universities tend to value traditional education over nontraditional options. Some professors who earned their degrees in traditional schools believe their way is the only way to a valid education. Higher education faculty and administrators are most often very "traditional" in their thinking of quality education. They tend to be less innovative, and less accepting of other methods of teaching than the traditional lecture/test format for learning.

If you are planning to advance your career in business or industry, the acceptance of a non-traditional Graduate program may be much greater. The ivy-league (pay for a pedigree) schools still carry weight when competing for executive level jobs. However, most often the importance is placed on the fact that you have a graduate degree, more so than where you earned it. Specialized companies, such as Engineering, may recruit heavily from certain Engineering schools. Ask your present, or potential employer for their suggestions for Graduate study – before you enroll in any program.

You will find information on many nontraditional graduate degrees in the Adult Learner Degree Programs section at the end of the book.

Whatever you final decision, graduate schools are competitive for admissions (getting in) and for graduation (getting out). The expectancy of performance is much greater than for undergraduate coursework. You will spend more time using research, and writing reports. However, the topics of study will be narrowed to your area of interest. Since the amount of courses needed for graduation is much less than an undergraduate degree – time will fly, and the next thing you know you will be graduating.

Take pride in <u>your</u> success.

Notes about this chapter:

GLOSSARY OF COLLEGE TERMS

Academic Advisor - A person who assists students in planning their educational program(s).

Associate Degrees - Degrees offered by two-year colleges, usually the A.A. (Associate of Arts), A.S. (Associate of Science), or A.A.S. (Associate of Applied Science). Often, courses in "Applied" areas are not as easily transferable.

Bachelor's Degree - Degrees offered by four-year colleges, usually the B.A. (Bachelor of Arts) or B.S. (Bachelor of Science).

Catalog - A publication that lists the academic policies and procedures of a college and includes descriptions of programs and courses.

Certificate - A credential awarded at a two-year institution for a course of study lasting a year or less.

Continuing Education - Any educational program whereby an adult may be retrained or upgraded in professional, or vocational skills. May also be referred to as adult education.

Credits - Units given for completion of any study that applies toward a college degree.

Curriculum - The body of courses required to earn a particular degree or certificate.

Degree Completion Program - An undergraduate degree that allows the student to maximize credits already earned, and knowledge acquired, in order to complete a degree in an accelerated fashion.

Degrees – Paper credential given to students who have successfully completed specified courses of study; usually associate degrees, bachelor's degrees, master's degrees, or doctoral degrees.

Department - Within a college; a unit that offers courses in a specific subject area or a specific group of subjects. For example, a history department might offer only courses in history; a social sciences department may offer courses in psychology, sociology, anthropology, history and other subjects.

Distribution Requirements, General Education, or Core - Terms used to describe the common body of foundation coursework that all students must take to complete any degree program.

Transfer or Dual Degree program - A cooperative degree between two institutions (usually a community college and a four-year college) whereby the student begins the coursework at one institution and completes it at another.

Elective - A student may select the course; the credits, but not the course are required to earn a degree or certificate.

Grade Point Average (GPA) - A number that ranges from 0.00 to 4.00 and indicates students' average course grades.

Lower Division - The first two years of college study: the freshman and sophomore years.

Mini-Mester, Mini-Term, January Term - A short, intensive term of study.

Prerequisite - A requirement that must be completed before a course may be taken. For example, the prerequisite for an intermediate algebra course may be a course in elementary algebra.

Quarter System - A system that divides a school year into three parts, usually a fall, winter and spring term-- often ten weeks each. A Summer Session is offered to conclude the quarters.

Semester System - A system that divides a school year into two parts, usually a fall and spring term often fifteen to sixteen weeks each. A Summer Session is offered to conclude the semesters.

Term - A period of study in a college. A term may be a semester, a quarter or a summer session, interim or other.

Transcripts - Official record of courses taken, grades received, and grade point averages.

Upper Division - The third and fourth years of study in a four-year college; courses with UD level designation.

RESOURCE DIRECTORY

Accreditation

Regional Accreditation Bureaus for Higher Education Institutions -

Middle States Association of Colleges and Schools
3624 Market Street
Philadelphia, PA 19104
(215) 662-5606
www.msche.org
(Accredits: Delaware, District of Columbia, Maryland, New Jersey, New York, Pennsylvania, Puerto Rico, the Republic of Panama, Virgin Islands, and several institutions in Europe serving primarily U.S. students)

New England Association of Schools and Colleges
209 Burlington Road
Bedford, MA 01730-1433
(617) 2710022
www.neasc.org
(Accredits: Connecticut, Maine, Massachusetts, New Hampshire, Rhode Island, Vermont.)

North Central Association of Colleges and Schools
30 North LaSalle Street, Suite 2400
Chicago, IL 60602
(312) 263-0456
www.nca.org
(Accredits: Arizona, Arkansas, Colorado, Illinois, Indiana, Iowa, Kansas, Michigan, Minnesota, Missouri, Nebraska, New Mexico, North Dakota, Ohio, Oklahoma, South Dakota, West Virginia, Wisconsin, Wyoming)

Northwest Association of Schools and Colleges
11130 NE 33rd Place, Station 120
Bellevue, WA 98004
(425) 827-2005
www.conasc.org
(Accredits: Alaska, Montana, Nevada, Oregon, Utah, Washington)

Southern Association of Colleges and Schools
1866 Southern Lane.
Decatur, GA 30033-4097
(404) 679-4500
www.sacscoc.org
(Accredits: Alabama, Florida, Georgia, Kentucky, Louisiana, Mississippi, North Carolina, South Carolina, Tennessee, Texas, Virginia)

Western Association of Schools and Colleges
3402 Mendocino Avenue
Santa Rosa, CA 95403-2244
(408) 688-7575
www.accjc.org

985 Atlantic Avenue, Station 100
Alameda, CA 94501
(510) 748-9001
www.wascweb.org/senior

(Accredits: American Samoa, California, Guam, Hawaii, Trust Territory of the Pacific)

Other Accrediting Bureaus

Accrediting Council for Independent Colleges and Schools (ACICS)
750 First Street, NE, Suite 980
Washington, D.C. 20002-4241
(202) 336-6780
www.acics.org

American Association of Bible Colleges (AABC)
5575 South Senoran Blvd., Station 26
Orlando, FL 32822-0840
(407) 207-0808
www.aabc.org

Association of Theological Schools in the U.S. and Canada (ATS)
10 Summit Park Drive
Pittsburgh, PA 15275-1103
(412) 788-6505
www.ats.edu

Distance Education and Training Council (DETC)
1601 18th Street, NW
Washington, DC 20009
(202) 234-5100
www.detc.org

Specialized Agencies & Organizations

American Association of Colleges and School of Business (AACSB)
600 Emerson Road, Station 300
St. Louis, MO 63141-6762
(314) 872-8481
www.aacsb.edu

American Council of Education (ACE)
One Dupont Circle
Washington, DC 20036-1193
(202) 939-9300
www.acenet.edu

American College Testing (ACT Exams)
2201 North Dodge Street
PO Box 168
2201 North Dodge Street
Iowa City, Iowa 52243-0168
(319) 337-1270
www.act.org

The College Board (SAT and CLEP Exams)
45 Columbus Avenue
New York, NY 10023-6992
(212) 713-8000
www.collegeboard.com

Community College of the Air Force
Maxwell Air Force Base
Montgomery, AL 36112-6655
(334) 953-6436
http://www.au.af.mil/au/ccaf

Educational Testing Services (ETS - GRE, GMAT Exams)
Rosedale Road
Princeton, NJ 08541
(609) 921-9000
www.ets.org

The Hay Group (LSI)
The Wanamaker Building
100 Penn Square East
Philadelphia, PA 19107-3388
(215) 861-2000
www.haygroup.com

National Program on Non-collegiate Sponsored Instruction (PONSI)
Education Building Addition, Room 960A
89 Washington Avenue
Albany, NY 12234
(518) 4486-2070
www.nationalponsi.org

Notes:

READING RESOURCES

American Council on Education, Ed. (2002). The Guide To The Evaluation Of Educational Experiences In The Armed Services. Greenwood Press: ACE/Praeger Series on Higher Education.

American Council on Education, Ed. (2002). The National Guide To Educational Credit For Training Programs. Greenwood Press: ACE/Praeger Series on Higher Education.

Bear, J., Bear M. (2003) Bear's Guide to Earning Degrees by Distance Learning. Ten Speed Press.

Bolles, R.N. (2003 edition). What Color Is Your Parachute? Berkeley: Ten Speed Press.

Carroll, J. L. (1997). College Credit Without Classes: How to Obtain Academic Credit for What You Already Know. Ferguson Publishing.

Carter, C., Bishop, J., Kravits, S.L., D'Agostino, J.V. (2001). Keys to College Studying: Becoming a Lifelong Learner. Pearson Education.

Gilbert, S. D. (2000). How to Be a Successful Online Student. The McGraw-Hill Companies.

Kramer, C. (2001). Success in Distance Learning. Delmar Learning.

Kolb, D.A. (1986). The Learning Styles Inventory. Boston: McBer & Company.

Siebert, A., Gilpin B., Karr, KM. (2000). Adult Student's Guide to Survival & Success. 4th Edition. Practical Psychology Press.

Simon, Linda (2001) New Beginnings: A Guide for Adult Learners. Pearson Education.

Smith, Laurence N. and Walter, Timothy L. (1994) The Adult Learner's Guide to College Success. Wadsworth Publishing.

Stevenson, Nancy (2000). Distance Learning Online for Dummies. Wiley, John & Sons, Inc.

Tieger, P.D., Barron-Tieger, B.,(2001). Do What You Are: Discover the Perfect Career for You through the Secrets of Personality Type. Brown & Little Company.

WEB/INTERNET RESOURCES

www.back2college.com   www.acenet.edu   www.adultstudent.com
www.pbs.org/als   www.ncld.org   www.utexas.edu/world/univ/state
http://adulted.about.com   www.ed.gov/index.jsp   www.supercollege.com
www.IRS.gov   www.finaid.org   www.careeronestop.org

Colleges & University Searches

New college web sites are being created almost daily. The quality of information available at these web sites varies widely, but most contain the college catalog and schedule of courses.

There are many "free" websites to search for colleges. But, remember, there are no "free lunches". These are some problems with "free" search sites:

1. If a site is "free" for the consumer, they are getting their revenues from the back end – they charge colleges to be in their database. Therefore, only the colleges that pay to be in the database can be found. The database is not comprehensive. There may be hundreds of excellent programs that are not listed in their "free" search.

2. Most all college searches include information that is pertinent to the traditionally-aged, young, college student – not adult learners. They do not have information for, and about, adult learner programs. Thus, the information is of no use to the adult student.

Suggestion: You may want to use our exclusive database designed solely for adult learners who are interested in the study fields of business. It contains all U.S. college/university programs for adult learners, including extended campus locations. **Go to: www.e-a-s.com and click-on the OnLine Advisor option.**

Financial Aid

It is very difficult for adult learners to receive financial-aid. All financial-aid applications require a statement of income, and declaration of investments, property and other assets which often place the adult learner out of any bracket for financial support. Here are some websites for information and help:

www.theoldschool.org   www.finaid.org/otheraid/older.phtml   http://adulted.about.com/cs/financialaid/

Tests & Test Preparation

The College Board Online has information on testing sites, schedules, and resources for test preparation and CLEP exams: www.collegeboard.org

Educational Testing Services maintains a general web site as well as sites for the GRE and GMAT tests: www.ets.org   www.mba.com

Kaplan Education Centers offer preparation courses for a variety of entrance exams: www.kaplan.com

The Princeton Review offers preparation courses for a variety of entrance exams: www.review.com

Moore Educational Publishers: www.istudysmart.com

ADULT LEARNER COLLEGE PROGRAMS

There are thousands of colleges/universities that offer specialized programs to meet the needs and learning styles of adult learners. Colleges spend millions on "recruiting – sales" efforts to enroll adults in their programs. Some colleges do an exceptional job of advertising – but, this does not mean they are the only, or best choice for you. Determine your own needs, and do your own research. Don't be "sold" into one of the most important and costly decision of your life – your education.

There are hundreds of college/universities that offer "Distance Learning" courses and degrees. It is estimated that about 85% of public universities offer non-residential distance learning courses, degrees, or career credentials. Private colleges/universities are often even more likely to have adult-centered programs with many options for credit, as they can quickly add/change their curriculums to meet demand. It is estimated that there are over 10,000 courses on the internet.

EASi does not accept any payment from colleges to be included in our database – The OnLine Advisor – nor for these program listings and information. Below is a listing of some of the renown, Regionally Accredited colleges/universities that offer programs for adults that can be taken via the classroom and/or distance learning:

CAPELLA UNIVERSITY – 222 South 9th Street, 20th Floor, Minneapolis, MN 55402. (888) CAPELLA. www.capella.edu. This institution of higher education which offers undergraduate and graduate degree programs, certificates, and continuing education to adult learners who seek to integrate advanced study with their professional lives. Its mission is to deliver high quality programs that provide traditional and contemporary knowledge through flexible and innovative forms of distance learning. Capella University explicitly recognizes adult learners as active partners in the design and implementation of their academic experience. All program are online; there are no campus locations.

> **Majors:** (undergraduate) Many majors and specializations to choose from their Schools of Technology, Psychology, Business, Education and Human Services on both undergraduate and graduate levels.
> **Certificates:** Availability changes; view their website.
> **Admissions:** (undergraduate) degree-completion program; must transfer approximately 60.0 semester credits of college work with at least a 2.0 GPA. (graduate) regionally accredited Bachelor degree and a GPA of at least 2.7. No exams listed.
> **ACE/PONSI Corporate And Military Credit:** ACE Military and Corporate credit.
> **Prior Learning Assessment:** Use the Capella Petition Center to get credit for your prior learning. Capella University grants credit for corporate training programs and business-related work experiences that are relevant to your academic program. Even if you have not earned a certificate or license, Capella can award credit for work experience and training through a Portfolio process.
> **Distance Learning:** All courses at Capella University are online. They are much like familiar, classroom-based courses. Learning takes place through a blend of assigned readings, class discussion, faculty feedback, group projects, case studies, research and writing assignments. You can expect to invest a minimum of 10 hours each week in a course, two or more hours of which will be devoted to online course-room discussions.
> **Testing:** CLEP, DANTES

CHARTER OAK STATE COLLEGE - 55 Paul J. Manafort Drive, New Britian, CT 06053. (860) 832-3800. www.cocs.edu. An external degree program designed especially for working adults. Charter Oak holds no classes. Instead, students earn credits from courses transferred from regionally accredited colleges and universities, testing, independently guided study, online and video courses, contract learning and assessment of prior learning. Degrees granted include associate and bachelor degrees in liberal arts and other areas.

Majors: Liberal Arts, Business, Computer Science, Fire Science, Individualized Studies, Industrial Technology, Technology & Management, Applied Science & Technology, others.

Certificates: Not available.

Admissions: Open to any person 16 years or older, regardless of level of formal education, who is able to demonstrate college-level achievement. To be admitted you must have earned nine college-level credits from any acceptable source. Submit high school (or GED) diploma and transcripts from previous colleges.

ACE/PONSI Corporate And Military Credit: The College grants credit for military and corporate training based on ACE recommendations. Other non-collegiate courses may be evaluated by Charter Oak State College.

Prior Learning Assessment: Credit may be awarded for learning acquired through life or work experience which is equivalent to learning acquired in courses offered by regionally accredited colleges and universities through the development of an educational portfolio.

Distance Learning: Credit may be earned through local college courses, correspondence courses offered by regionally accredited institutions, Charter Oak Independent Guided Study courses and contract learning.

Testing: Grants credit for CLEP, ACT PEP, GRE, Advanced Placement, & DANTES

CITY UNIVERSITY – 11900 NE First Street, Bellevue, WA 98005. (888) 42CITYU. www.cityu.edu
Private, nonprofit institution of higher education founded more than two decades ago to serve working adults wanting to pursue educational opportunities without interrupting their careers. The University's mission is to provide educational opportunities world wide.

Majors: City University offers more than 50 programs at the undergraduate and graduate levels. These programs cover a variety of academic fields ranging from business management and technology to counseling and teacher preparation. The university's Master of Business Administration and Master of Education degree programs are among the largest in the nation.

Certificates: Many options on both the Undergraduate and Graduate levels. Accounting, C& C++ Programming, Financial Management, Human Resource Management, Marketing, Networking/Telecommunications, Project management, Web Design & Languages, e-Commerce.

Admissions: Admission is available continuously throughout the year. Submit high school (or GED) Diploma and transcripts from previous colleges. No SAT or ACT is required. Graduate admissions require that students hold a baccalaureate degree or equivalent from an accredited or otherwise recognized institution. No specific undergraduate emphasis or major is required for entrance into a particular graduate program. If available, reported scores on standardized entrance examinations such as the GRE, the MAT, and the GMAT should be submitted, although these are not required. Check with department for additional requirements.

ACE/PONSI Corporate And Military Credit: The University grants credit for military and corporate training as recommended by ACE.

Prior Learning Assessment: Students may earn college credits for learning acquired through documented experiential learning through the Prior Learning Experience (PLE) program. Students prepare a portfolio by enrolling in the PLE Preparation course. Undergraduate degree candidates may earn up to 45 credits by means of a PLE portfolio. Associate's degree candidates may earn up to 23 credits through the portfolio.

Distance Learning: The distance learning option makes available most of the university's degree and certificate programs entirely by independent study. Students order a study guide, textbooks, and where necessary, other instructional materials from the University bookstore. Students study independently, and remain in contact with their instructors via mail, phone or computer link. Good student services policies, and keeping in touch with students.

Testing: City University participates in several of the nationally recognized standardized testing programs, including CLEP, ACT-PEP, USAFI/DANTES, Advanced Placement and the Certified Professional Secretary Examination.

COLORADO STATE UNIVERSITY – Division of Continuing Education, Spruce Hall, Fort Collins, CO 80523-1040.(970) 491-1101.www.welcome.colostate.edu. A large, traditional, public university provides evening classes in Ft. Collins, and a Denver campus. They have an extensive distance learning program with video-based, and online courses for certificate, undergraduate degree-completion, and graduate education for working professionals who cannot attend on-campus classes. The SURGE (State University Resources in Graduate Education) program consists of regular on-campus courses that are videotaped. The tapes, along with handouts, are sent via UPS on a weekly basis. Interaction with the instructor is possible through electronic mail, FAX, computer communication, surface mail, and telephone. There is no on-campus residency requirement to complete a master's degree. The Ph.D. requires at least two academic semesters on campus.

> **Majors:** Many programs are offered via classroom and various locations within Colorado. There are only a few undergraduate majors via distance learning – Social Sciences, Fire Science Management, and Information Science & Technology. Most of their distance programs are on the Graduate level – MBA, Engineering, Computer Science, Telecommunications, Education, others.
> **Certificates:** Data Analysis, Finance, Information Science, Project Management, others.
> **Admissions:** Submit high school (or GED) diploma and transcripts from previous colleges.
> **ACE/PONSI Corporate And Military Credit:** Possible military credit.
> **Prior Learning Assessment:** No Portfolio process available.
> **Distance Learning:** Telecourses Courses are videotaped and shipped to students with other course materials. Students take examinations under the supervision of a local proctor. (Correspondence) The University offers selected undergraduate, graduate and non-credit correspondence courses through the Colorado Consortium for Independent Study via Correspondence. No degrees are available completely through correspondence.
> **Testing:** CLEP, DANTES

DEVRY COLLEGE- One Tower Lane, Oakbrook Terrace, IL 60181. (800) 73-DEVRY. www.devry.edu. This college offers career-oriented education that applies directly to the workplace in fields of Business. They have campuses located nationwide with ongoing career support. Their programs give you the technical knowledge and hands-on experience you need to follow the future's most promising paths. They have accelerated courses for quicker degree completion.

> **Majors:** (associate) Business, Engineering Technology fields, Electronic fields, Network Systems Administration, Technical Management, Telecommunications Management. (bachelor) Business, Engineering Technology fields, Electronics Engineering, Information Technology, Technical Management, Telecommunications Management. (graduate programs are through their Keller School of Management – see below).
> **Certificates:** Accounting Finance, Information Technology, Project Management, others.
> **Admissions:** Submit high school (or GED) diploma and transcripts from previous colleges.
> **ACE/PONSI Corporate And Military Credit:** ACE Military credit.
> **Prior Learning Assessment:** Not available.
> **Distance Learning:** In addition to its campus facilities across North America, DeVry offers online learning, which integrates today's high-tech Internet-based capabilities with DeVry's proven educational methodologies. Student academic performance for online courses is assessed via thorough evaluation of contributions to team/group activities, participation in threaded discussions and performance on individual assignments, projects, papers and case studies. By combining these activities with results from online quizzes and proctored exams, instructors build complete portfolios reflecting students' mastery of course objectives. In addition to offering high-quality education online, DeVry is committed to providing online students with access to a full range of support services.
> **Testing:** CLEP, DANTES.

DEVRY COLLEGE- KELLER GRADUATE SCHOOL OF MANAGEMENT. One Tower Lane, Oakbrook Terrace, IL 60181. (800) 73-DEVRY. www.devry.edu. This college offers career-oriented education that applies directly to the workplace in fields of Business. They have campuses located nationwide with ongoing career support. Their programs give you the technical knowledge and hands-on experience you need to follow the future's most promising paths. They have accelerated courses for quicker degree completion.

Majors: (graduate) MBA, Accounting & Financial Management, Human Resource Management, Information Systems Management, Project Management, Public Administration, Telecommunications Management.

Certificates: (graduate level) Accounting, Business Administration, Educational Management, Electronic Commerce Management, Entrepreneurship, Financial Analysis, Health Services Management, Human Resource Management, Information Security, Information Systems Management, Project Management, Telecommunications Management.

Admissions: Undergraduate degree. GRE, GMAT or institutional exam. Some pre-requisite courses. computer competency, others.

ACE/PONSI Corporate And Military Credit: Not applicable.

Prior Learning Assessment: Not available

Distance Learning: Our approach to distance learning integrates today's high-tech capabilities with proven instructional methodologies. The result is solid education enhanced by the latest in interactive information technology – online class discussion groups, CDs, e-mail, online classroom lectures, additional Internet resources, as well as traditional textbooks – that enables students to send and receive feedback from instructors, as well as to participate in various group and team. Almost all majors listed above are available online.

EMPIRE STATE COLLEGE - One Union Avenue, Saratoga Springs, NY 12866. (518) 587-2100. www.esc.edu. This college is expressly dedicated to offering high-quality education for working adults for both the Undergraduate and Graduate degree levels.

Majors: (undergraduate) Has a wide range of degrees and programs that you can customize to your needs and goals. You can also design a program of study with their "Learning Contract" from their 11 areas of study. (graduate) Business Policy, Labor Studies, Liberal Studies, Social Policy, MBA.

Certificates: Labor Management, Information Systems, others.

Admissions: Requirements vary considerably between selected majors, campus study, and distance learning options on both the Undergraduate and Graduate levels.

ACE/PONSI Corporate And Military Credit: Corporate and Military credit for ACE.

Prior Learning Assessment: Personal mentor to help students complete a Portfolio.

Distance Learning: Associate and Bachelor programs – Human Services, Business, Management, Economics, Health Services, Marketing; may be others.

Testing: CLEP, DANTES, Challenge, T-CEP, Excelsior College Exams.

EXCELSIOR COLLEGE - 7 Columbia Circle, Albany, NY 12203-5159. (888) 647-2388. www.excelsior.edu. A public, non-traditional college offering associate and bachelor's degrees through a variety of distance learning options, including credit for life experience, standardized examinations, correspondence courses and other distance learning options. Very accessible to adults.

Majors: Many areas of study including Business, Nursing, Technology and Liberal Arts for either Associate or Bachelor level degrees. Includes – Accounting, Management, Human Services, and International Business, Human Resources, Operations Management, Marketing, others.

Certificates: Not available.

Admissions: Submit high school (or GED) diploma and transcripts from previous colleges.

ACE/PONSI Corporate And Military Credit: Grants credit for corporate and military training as recommended by ACE/PONSI.

Prior Learning Assessment: Not available directly with Excelsior, but through selected colleges.

Distance Learning: Offers correspondence and online courses, which may include textbooks, workbooks, course guides, video programs, audio-cassettes, computer programs and similar resources. Students work under the guidance of a faculty tutor.

Testing: Recognizes credits earned through approved testing programs such as CLEP, DANTES, Excelsior College Examinations, and the Thomas Edison Testing Program.

FIELDING GRADUATE INSTITUTE – 2112 Santa Barbara Street, Santa Barbara, CA 93105. (805) 687 - 1099. www.fielding.edu. An institution of graduate study based on the principles of adult learning. Within curriculum guidelines and requirement, students can negotiate the means by which they acquire and demonstrate their knowledge. Students are encouraged to exercise initiative, both in proposing individualization within curriculum guidelines, and in selecting the combination of study procedures that is best adapted to their learning styles. Students collaborate with faculty members who advise and evaluate adherence to established academic standards. Degrees offered include master's and doctoral degree programs.

> **Majors:** Clinical Psychology, Human & Organization Development, Education, others.
> **Certificates:** Graduate level. Organizational Management, Leadership, Virtual Teams, others.
> **Admissions:** Applicants must possess a bachelor's or master's degree from a regionally accredited institution with a minimum GPA of 3.0 for the highest degree. No admissions tests are required. Additional requirements depend on individual circumstances.
> **ACE/PONSI Corporate And Military Credit:** Not applicable.
> **Prior Learning Assessment:** Not applicable.
> **Distance Learning:** All course work is done independently with close contact between the student and faculty. A variety of methods may be used such as "cluster" classrooms or web-casts.
> **Testing:** Not applicable.

JONES INTERNATIONAL UNIVERSITY- (formerly Mind Extension University) 9687 East Mineral Avenue P O BOX 6612, Englewood, CO 80155-8612. (800) 777 – MIND. www.jonesinternational.edu. JIU was the first Web-based university to exist entirely online. They offer courses and degree programs from more than 30 regionally accredited universities through cable television and the internet. Degrees available include Bachelor's, and master's levels. Some certificate programs are also available.

> **Majors:** (Bachelor) Business Administration, Information Technology, Business Communications. (Master) MBA, Education, Business Communications.
> **Certificates:** Many. Financial Management, Information Technology, Entrepreneurship, others.
> **Admissions:** Rather open admissions for undergraduate; graduate dependent on department. Will transfer credits from a DETC (vocational) school.
> **ACE/PONSI Corporate And Military Credit:** Military credit has been given.
> **Prior Learning Assessment:** Credits granted for both undergraduate and graduate programs.
> **Distance Learning:** All courses available through cable television and online/internet.
> **Testing:** CLEP, DANTES.

NATIONAL- LOUIS UNIVERSITY - 1000 Capitol Drive, Wheeling, Il. 60090. (847) 465-0575. www.nl.edu. For more than a century, National-Louis University has served those who serve others. The institution was founded as National College of Education in 1886 by Elizabeth Harrison, a pioneer in elementary and early childhood education. Another rapid growth area, business programs, culminated with the formation in 1989 of the College of Management and Business. The institutional name, National-Louis University, unites the great name of National College of Education with that of trustee and benefactor Michael W. Louis. Classes are scheduled by location, cohort programs, and distance education.

> **Majors:** (undergraduate) Accounting, Business Administration, Computer Information Systems, English, Human Services, Education, Liberal Arts Studies, Psychology, Math/Quantitative Studies. (graduate) Many fields of Education, Psychology. Written Communications, MBA, Managerial Leadership, Human Resource Management & Development.
> **Certificates:** IT Certifications, Assurance, others.
> **Admissions:** (undergraduate) high school transcript or college transcript(s). (graduate) Bachelor degree transcripts; GRE, GMAT writing sections, MAT, or institutional exam in writing skills; letters of reference.
> **ACE/PONSI Corporate And Military Credit:** Military and Corporate ACE credit.
> **Prior Learning Assessment:** Portfolio credit possible for all degrees.
> **Distance Learning:** Almost all degrees and levels available online.
> **Testing:** CLEP, DANTES, Excelsior/PEP exams.

NATIONAL TECHNICAL UNIVERSITY - 155 Fifth Avenue South, Suite 600, Minneapolis, MN 55401. (800) 582-9976. www.ntu.edu. Offers graduate-level degree programs and for-credit courses in engineering, management, and computer-related fields, as well as non-credit professional development courses through a consortium of over 50 U.S. college and universities. Contracts with many corporations for onsite programs.

    Majors: Information Systems, Project Management, Engineering fields, MBA, Telecommunications, Software, Computer Engineering, Environmental Systems, Software Engineering, others.

    Certificates: Hundreds of Professional Development courses and certificate programs, in Business and Engineering fields of study.

    Admissions: Varies a bit with selected degree program. Most Bachelor degrees must be from an ABET college/university rating.

    ACE/PONSI Corporate and Military Credit: Not applicable.

    Prior Learning Assessment: Not applicable; some transfer credit awarded.

    Distance Learning: videotapes, webcasts, online courses, CD-ROM courses.

    Tests: Very limited; possibly through Challenge Exams.

NOVA SOUTHEASTERN UNIVERSITY - 3301 College Avenue, Fort Lauderdale, FL 33314. (800) 541-6682. www.nova.edu. A private, not-for-profit independent institution dedicated to providing high-quality educational programs of distinction from pre-school through the professional and doctoral levels, as well as service to the community. It offers academic programs at times convenient to students, employing innovative delivery systems and rich learning resources on campus and at distant sites with "cluster" classrooms and through their Student Education Centers located in many metro cities across the U.S.

    Majors: (AA/BA/BS) Early Childhood Education, Nursing, Health Science. Many other programs offer at their home campus. (Graduate) Many programs on campus – Audiology, Business, Computer Information Sciences, Criminal Justice, Education, Various Medical degrees, others.

    Certificates: Workshops, not certificate programs.

    Admissions: Varies with program of study. Graduate School requires a bachelor's or master's degree from a regionally accredited institution. Contact department for additional requirements.

    ACE/PONSI Corporate and Military Credit: Some credits may be granted.

    Prior Learning Assessment: Available for undergraduate degrees, after taking course with NOVA. Potential transfer credit for vocational school transcripts.

    Distance Learning: A variety of distance learning methods, including regional cluster groups are used to meet degree requirements. These are actual classrooms; not internet courses. Many more degree options than on their home campus for Bachelor, Master's, Doctoral levels in the fields of – Business, Technology, Psychology, Education, Allied Health, Humanities & Social Science, others.

    Testing: CLEP, DANTES, others.

OHIO UNIVERSITY - External Student Program – Hanning Hall, Athens, OH 45701. (800) 444-2910. www.ohiou.edu. For more than 100 years, part of the mission of Ohio University has been to extend learning opportunities beyond its classrooms.. The programs and services of the Division of Lifelong Learning are integrated into the fabric of the university, drawing upon the strength of its faculty and curriculum to maintain a tradition of excellence. Classes are also offered on campus and at a few other sites.

    Majors: Extensive list of majors, including a Bachelor of Specialized Studies which allows you to integrate
various departmental courses, and design your curriculum.

    Certificates: Few

    Admissions: Submit high school (or GED) diploma and transcripts from previous colleges. Transfer students must have a minimum cumulative GPA of 2.0. No admissions test required.

    ACE/PONSI Corporate and Military Credit: Credit for both military and corporate ACE training.

    Prior Learning Assessment: One of the few public institutions that provide this option. Students may earn credit for learning from on-the-job training, seminars, workshops, volunteer work, hobbies, reading, or other learning experiences. Students enroll in a four-hour independent study course to prepare a portfolio documenting learning experiences.

Distance Learning: Course-delivery options include print, audio- and videotape, computers, compact disks, and the Internet and world Wide Web. Students submit assignments by postal mail, fax, and e-mail.

Testing: Grants credit by institutional Challenge examination for a wide variety of courses. The University also grants credit for CLEP subject examinations.

PENNSYLVANIA STATE UNIVERSITY – Adult Student Programs – 201 Shields Building, Box 3000, University Park, PA 16804-3000. (814) 865-5471. www.psu.edu. Offers more than 300 courses, including certificate and associate degree programs through independent study. Textbooks, study guides and other materials (including video and audiotapes for some courses) are mailed to the students. Communicate with the instructors by mail and telephone. Their extended campuses reach to over 22 sites/cities throughout Pennsylvania.

> **Majors:** (undergraduate) Has over 160 different majors to choose; will vary if offered at the home-campus, other locations or via distance learning – Liberal Arts, Organizational Leadership, others. (graduate) Adult Education, MBA, Curriculum & Instruction; possibly others.
>
> **Certificates:** Many and with wide variety – Business, Communications, Family Services, Dietary, Adult Development, Hospitality Management, Human Resources, Customer Relations, others.
>
> **Admissions:** Degree candidates must be admitted into the Penn State degree program by the admissions office. Some degrees require a placement examination, or Graduate entry exam.
>
> **ACE/PONSI Corporate and Military Credit:** Accepts both military and corporate ACE training.
>
> **Prior Learning Assessment**: A currently enrolled student who can document college-level learning acquired in a non-collegiate setting (such as work or volunteer experience, a training program, or a hobby) may be able to petition for undergraduate credit through portfolio assessment. Not all academic units will consider these requests. Consequently, students interested in determining whether to pursue credit by portfolio assessment opportunities should contact the academic department responsible for the relevant course.
>
> **Distance Learning**: All courses available through correspondence and online/internet.
>
> **Testing:** CLEP, DANTES, others.

TEXAS UNIVERSITY SYSTEM – 601 Colorado Street, Austin, TX 78701-2982. (512) 499-4200. www.utsystem.edu. The core commitment of The University of Texas System is to provide education as a life-transforming experience. They have 15 component institutions which are composed of thousands of people that are making a difference in Texas and in the global community. These campuses are located throughout the state of Texas, and most all offer programs for adult learners via classroom and/or distance learning. The UT institutions provide superior instruction and learning opportunities to 169,635 undergraduate, graduate and professional school students from a wide range of soial, ethnic, cultural, and economic backgrounds.

> **Majors:** The UT system campuses offer hundreds of majors on the undergraduate and graduate levels, in the fields of Business, Social Work, Liberal Arts, Health Sciences, Nursing, Public Affairs, Law, Engineering, Sciences, Fine Arts, Education, Architecture, Social Sciences, Communications, and many others.
>
> **Certificates:** None listed.
>
> **Admissions:** To take a classroom-based or an online course for credit via the UTTC, you must apply and be admitted to a UT campus. Each campus has the same admission standards and process; more traditional requirements. Same faculty that teach classroom teach distance courses.
>
> **ACE/PONSI Corporate And Military Credit:** None listed.
>
> **Prior Learning Assessment:** No Portfolio options.
>
> **Distance Learning:** Degree programs are more limited through the UT Tele Campuses and online courses. Most are on the graduate level – MBA, Curriculum & Instruction, Computer Science, Engineering, Public Administration, Human Resources, others. Some programs may be on an accelerated format.
>
> **Testing:** CLEP

THOMAS EDISON STATE COLLEGE - 101 West State Street, Trenton, NJ 08608-1176. (888) 442-8372. www.tesc.edu. A public institution offering 14 Associate, Baccalaureate, and Master's degrees to students from every state in the U.S. and 86 countries around the world. Students earn degrees through a variety of rigorous academic methods, including a variety of distance education methods such as documenting college-level knowledge they may already have and by completing independent study courses. The college offers no classroom instruction and has no residency requirement.

> **Majors:** Many available with a wide range of study – (associate & bachelor) Business, Technology, Human Services, Health Sciences, Nursing, Natural Sciences, others. (graduate) Business, Project Management, Technology, Substance Abuse, Liberal Arts, others.
>
> **Certificates:** Many available – Accounting, Office Management, Computers, eCommerce, Electronics, Fitness, Labor Studies Human Resources, Marketing, others.
>
> **Admissions:** Submit high school (or GED) diploma and transcripts from previous colleges. No admissions test is required. Differences vary for graduate study.
>
> **ACE/PONSI Corporate and Military Credit:** Grants credit for corporate or military training based on ACE/PONSI recommendations. The college has also evaluated many licenses and certificates for college credit.
>
> **Prior Learning Assessment:** The College evaluates skills and knowledge acquired from work experience, volunteer activities, training programs, hobbies, religious activities, homemaking skills, independent reading and special accomplishments through portfolio assessment.
>
> **Distance Learning:** All programs offered by the College are available through the widest possible variety of distance learning options **– (Correspondence) -** Under the Center for Directed Independent Adult Learning (DIAL), Guided Study courses are available to students. course work is completed independently by the students during a 16 or 24-week semester. Each course is structured around weekly readings, video and/or audio tapes and written assignments. Students receive written feedback from a faculty mentor, as well as the opportunity to telephone the mentor if needed. **(Telecourse)** The College is one of 60 colleges nationwide selected by the Public Broadcasting System as a partner in its *Going the Distance* program. Through the program the College offers courses on public television or VCR cassette. **(Computer)** The On-Line Computer Classroom uses computer communication to link distance learners with each other and their faculty mentors. Students attend class weekly by computer, discuss questions through a computer conference and submit written assignments on e-mail.
>
> **Testing:** The college offers more than 400 examinations for evaluating students' prior knowledge, including the CLEP general and subject examinations, ACT/PEP, USAFI/DANTES, Advanced Placement, and the Thomas Edison College Examination Program (TECEP) and others.

UNION INSTITUTE & UNIVERSITY- 440 E McMillan Street, Cincinnati, OH 45206-1947. (800) 486-3116. www.tui.edu. Originated nearly 40 years ago as a consortium of institutions, including Bard and Sarah Lawrence colleges, that united to form academically rigorous but convenient degree programs for adults. Plans of study are individually tailored. There are no prescribed courses. Each learner's program is developed in consultation with faculty advisors and other resource persons. Students must attend some periodic on-campus classes and/or activities. Extended campus sites include: Miami, Sacramento, Los Angeles, Cincinnati, Vermont.

> **Majors:** (undergraduate) Design your own degree or use established concentrations in – Criminal Justice, Business Management, Human Resources, Child Health, Social Work, Psychology, others. (graduate) Education, Fine Arts, Psychology, doctoral degree are interdisciplinary and students work with faculty to design their own course of study.
>
> **Certificates:** Wide variety; varies each term.
>
> **Admissions:** Admission depends on intelligence, creativity, demonstrated capacity for self-direction, and disciplined effort toward self-chosen objectives. Preference is given to those whose applications reflect strong potential for individual and professional growth and contribution to society. A master's degree is normally required of applicants, although an occasional exception may be made. No standardized tests are required.

ACE/PONSI Corporate and Military Credit: Accepts both military and corporate ACE training.
Prior Learning Assessment: Portfolio or life experience credits are possible.
Distance Learning: All programs of study may be completed at a distance.
Testing: CLEP, institutional Challenge exams.

UNIVERSITY OF CALIFORNIA /BERKLEY – Extension Programs - Berkeley, CA 95720. (510) 642-6000. www.berkeley.edu. From its inception 20 years after the California Gold Rush, UC faculty and students have looked to cross the horizons of what we know about our selves and our world, and what we can do in it. UC researchers are pioneers in agriculture, medicine, technology and the environment. UC is also actively involved in locations beyond its campuses, national labs and medical centers museums, concert halls, observatories, marine centers and botanical gardens - in places throughout California, around the world.

> **Majors:** UC/B has over 130 departments of study for Business, Sciences, Engineering, Education, Journalism, Public Health, Information Systems, and many more. They offer extensive distance learning options and over 7 classroom locations throughout California with evening and weekend courses.
>
> **Certificates:** Wide variety of subject areas – Accounting, Art, Drug Abuse, Business Administration, Data Warehousing, Career Planning, Computer Information Systems, Education Therapy, Facilities Planning, Finance, Human Resources, Garden Design, Marketing, Technology, others.
>
> **Admissions:** Adults follow the same traditional requirements as the younger students. Very competitive for Graduate study.
>
> **ACE/PONSI Corporate and Military Credit:** Not available.
>
> **Prior Learning Assessment:** Not available.
>
> **Distance Learning:** Since 1913, they offer hundreds of lower- and upper-division credit courses in a wide variety of fields including biological and physical sciences, computer science, film, health, history, math, natural sciences, social sciences, and writing. Instruction includes the use of computer technologies, correspondence courses, audio and video course delivery formats. Some courses are accelerated. About a half million students enroll with the Extension Center.
>
> **Testing:** CLEP, DANTES

UNIVERSITY OF IDAHO - Engineering Outreach, Janssen Engineering Building, Moscow, ID 83844-1014. (800) 824-2889. www. The University of Idaho offers extensive engineering degrees through extended campuses throughout Idaho and nationally through their Engineering Outreach program. They offer formats using telecommunications technology to deliver courses to distant student. Courses are taught on-campus, videotaped and sent anywhere to students. They also have a instate television system to broadcast courses. Additional courses are offered via correspondence and online.

> **Majors:** Graduate study in Engineering, Education, others.
>
> **Certificates:** Electric Machines, Secure Computing Systems, Materials Design, Communication Systems, Structural Engineering, Power Systems, Heating/Venting/Air Conditioning, others.
>
> **Admissions:** Applicants must have a bachelor's degree from an accredited college or university with a cumulative GPA of 2.8 or higher. Different departments have different requirements.
>
> **ACE/PONSI Corporate And Military Credit:** Military credit towards an undergraduate degree.
>
> **Prior Learning Assessment:** Not available.
>
> **Distance Learning:** Many undergraduate and graduate online courses. Videotaped courses are mailed to students each week. Localized television programming with many courses.
>
> **Testing:** CLEP

UNIVERSITY OF PHOENIX – 4615 East Elwood, Phoenix, AZ 85040. (800) MY-SUCCESS. www.phoenix.edu. Founded in 1976, is a private, for-profit higher education institution whose mission is to educate working adults to develop the knowledge and skills that will enable them to achieve their professional goals, improve the productivity of their organizations, and provide leadership and service to their communities.

The University educational philosophy and operational structure embody participative, collaborative, and applied problem solving strategies that are facilitated by a faculty whose advanced academic preparation and professional experience help integrate academic theory and current practical application. Uses classroom-based learning, online courses, and other methods. Currently has over 125 locations throughout the U.S., Canada and Puerto Rico.

Majors: Variety of fields of study. (undergraduate) Health Care Services, Education areas of study, Business, Accounting, eBusiness, Management, Marketing, Purchasing, Technology Systems. (graduate) Many area of Business, Technology Systems, Health Care, Nursing, Criminal Justice, Human Services, Counseling, others.

Certificates: Many; varies with location or online programs – MicroSoft Certifications, Business, Management, Auditor, Engineer, Cisco Certifications, Human Resources (SHRM), Mediation, Technology, Education, others.

Admissions: Almost an open-admission philosophy. Submit high school or college transcripts. Students are required to have significant work experience. Graduate applicants must have an undergraduate GPA of 2.5 and may be required to take the MAT or other graduate admissions examination.

ACE/PONSI Corporate and Military Credit: Grants credit for corporate or military training based on ACE recommendations.

Prior Learning Assessment: At the undergraduate level, awards credit for prior learning based on preparation of a portfolio. A class for Assessment of Prior Learning helps students prepare the portfolio.

Distance Learning: Has classroom locations all over the country; OnLine University offers extensive list of degree programs and courses.

TESTING: Grants credit for CLEP/DANTES, TECEP, other examinations.

Notes:

ABOUT THE AUTHOR

Dr. E. Faith Ivery founded Educational Advisory Services, Inc.® (EASi) (**www.e-a-s.com**) in 1981 in Denver, Colorado. She is currently President of EASi, which remains the nation's leading educational brokering firm. EASi has helped thousands of adult learners achieve their college degrees in a more efficient and cost-effective ways. Presently, EASi's corporate customer list includes of 40 Fortune 1000 level companies. She has worked nationally with adult learners in industry and higher education for over 20 years. Dr. Ivery is an expert on learning styles, learning options and academic advising models and programming. She is also a leader in supporting lifelong learning resources and developing cost-effective educational brokering programs. Her experience has taken her across the country as a workshop leader for adult learners and corporate Human Resources professionals. Dr.Ivery earned her Ed.D. degree from the University of Northern Colorado, in Educational Administration and College Student Personnel Administration with a specialization in the adult corporate learner and advising models. She earned her Master's degree at the University of Denver in Human Development Counseling, and her Bachelor's at the University of Florida in Psychology. Dr. Ivery earned her graduate degrees as a nontraditional adult learner.

Tribute To Sharon Lynn Kirk, Ed.D.   Since the first edition of this book, Dr. Sharon L. Kirk lost her battle with cancer in 1997. She was the student services counselor at Colorado Mountain College, Summit Campus. She had also worked as an Advisor for Metropolitan State College and Regis College – both in Denver. She advised students of all ages about financial aid, career choices, re-training, and degree completion. In youth, Sharon received a Liberal Arts degree from Monmouth College, Illinois; while teaching and parenting. Later she earned an M.A. in Counseling and Guidance from George Washington University, Washington, D.C., and, while in mid-career, an Ed.D in Educational Administration and College Student Personnel Administration from the University of Northern Colorado. As a lifelong learner Sharon was an advocate of the philosophy that " you can learn anything, at any age, and in any location with support."

Sharon was a joy to work with, and to call a dear friend. She fought her illness as hard as she fought for the "right" in all aspects of life. Of course, she was one of those special people that we all lose too soon. Her devotion to education and students of all ages was a lifelong endeavor. She was a loving wife and mother to two wonderful children, who are now grown and carry with them her positive influence. She was a true friend – lots of laughs, fun, tears and a tremendous support to me, and others, through life and learning. She made a difference in the lives of thousands of students, family and friends. This book is dedicated to her memory.

****

If you have any questions regarding the materials in this guidebook, would like to offer suggestions to enhance the contents for future editions, or need to order additional copies, EASi would be grateful for your input. You may write or call: Educational Advisory Services Inc., 10505 North 69th Street, Suite #1300, Scottsdale, AZ 85253. (480) 922-8986. www.E-A-S.com

If your employer has a Tuition Assistance Plan, and would like to obtain more accountability for the money spent on employee education, please call our office. Our professional educational planning service has proven to reduce the cost for a college degree by 20% or more, while aiding adult learners. This savings is passed on to the corporate TAP budget – and helps support corporate learning needs.

Order additional copies of *How to Earn a College Degree When You Think You Are Too Old, Too Busy, Too Broke, Too Scared* from Barnes & Noble – retail stores, by phone, or through their online bookstore at <u>www.barnesandnoble.com</u>. Volume discounts may apply.